What is Russia Up To
in the Middle East?

D0562079

Dmitri Trenin

———

What is Russia Up To in the Middle East?

polity

Copyright © Dmitri Trenin, 2018

The right of Dmitri Trenin to be identified as Author of this Work has been asserted in accordance with the UK Copyright, Designs and Patents Act 1988.

First published in 2018 by Polity Press
Reprinted 2018 (three times), 2019

Polity Press
65 Bridge Street
Cambridge CB2 1UR, UK

Polity Press
101 Station Landing, Suite 300
Medford, MA 02155, USA

ISBN-13: 978-1-5095-2230-9
ISBN-13: 978-1-5095-2231-6(pb)

A catalogue record for this book is available from the British Library.

Library of Congress Cataloging-in-Publication Data

Names: Trenin, Dmitrii, author.
Title: What is Russia up to in the Middle East? / Dmitri Trenin.
Description: 1 | Cambridge, UK ; Malden, MA : Polity, 2017. | Includes
    bibliographical references and index.
Identifiers: LCCN 2017013099 (print) | LCCN 2017035139 (ebook) | ISBN
    9781509522330 (Mobi) | ISBN 9781509522347 (Epub) | ISBN 9781509522309
    (hardback) | ISBN 9781509522316 (paperback)
Subjects: LCSH: Russia (Federation)--Foreign relations--Middle East. | Middle
    East)--Foreign relations--Russia (Federation) | World politics--1989- |
    BISAC: POLITICAL SCIENCE / Globalization.
Classification: LCC DK68.5 (ebook) | LCC DK68.5 .T74 2017 (print) | DDC
    327.47056--dc23
LC record available at https://lccn.loc.gov/2017013099

Typeset in 11 on 15 Sabon by
Servis Filmsetting Ltd, Stockport, Cheshire
Printed and bound in Great Britain by CPI Group (UK) Ltd, Croydon

The publisher has used its best endeavours to ensure that the URLs for external websites referred to in this book are correct and active at the time of going to press. However, the publisher has no responsibility for the websites and can make no guarantee that a site will remain live or that the content is or will remain appropriate.

Every effort has been made to trace all copyright holders, but if any have been inadvertently overlooked the publisher will be pleased to include any necessary credits in any subsequent reprint or edition.

For further information on Polity, visit our website:
politybooks.com

To Vera, for making my life fun and worth living

Contents

Acknowledgments

The idea for this book came up in a conversation with my Polity publisher, Dr. Louise Knight. Louise encouraged me to take up what was then, in the wake of the Russian military intervention in Syria, a very topical issue, expand on it, and put it into the proper regional and global context. Throughout my work on this short book, I felt constant assistance and support from Louise Knight and assistant editor Nekane Tanaka Galdos. I am very thankful to the reviewers—who will remain unknown to me—who first assessed the idea of the project, and then critiqued—and criticized—the manuscript. I am also indebted to Eric Schramm, who edited the final text.

Last but not least, I thank my wife, Vera, for her understanding, good humor, and patience with me, particularly during weekends on the dacha as I was holed up in my study writing this short book.

Introduction

The Syrian civil war is a defining moment in the contemporary history of the Middle East as much as the 2003 U.S.-led invasion of Iraq. Like Iraq, Syria also has global consequences. The U.S. capture of Baghdad and the removal of Saddam Hussein from power was the high-water mark of U.S. post–Cold War global dominance. It became a symbol of Washington's capacity to take and execute, single-handedly, virtually any decision affecting anyone in the world—even, if needed, against the opinion of all other members of the international community. America was truly unbound as a foreign policy actor, unlike any other country in history. Then, a series of recent developments, from the 2008 global financial crisis to the Arab Spring to the Ukrainian crisis to the Syrian war, marked the end of that unique position and ushered in a more familiar pattern of several large countries of unequal size and power vying for influence and for their preferred concept of world order.

The Middle East is a microcosm of these developments, and is as good a model as any for twenty-first-century power games changing the global balance. The "usual suspects"—those who for the past hundred years repeatedly intervened in the region, divided it into spheres of influence or sought to manipulate sociopolitical processes there—above all, the United States and its Western European allies—have grown weary, disillusioned, and progressively disinterested. In the process, they lost both the strategic initiative and the sense of direction. Curiously, the country that has been on the ascendance, economically, for the past four decades, China, is not yet eager to plunge into the waters of global geopolitics, and is only testing those waters. Another emerging great power, India, is even farther behind. Most strikingly, one major player, which had been virtually absent from the region—and the world—for the past quarter-century, Russia, is unexpectedly back in the game, and with gusto.

Moscow, of course, has not supplanted Washington as the principal actor or main security provider in the Middle East. It has no interest, no resources, and no intention to claim that role. What it has done instead is to have broken out of its post-Soviet condition of being essentially preoccupied with the former imperial borderlands and largely absent from the rest of the world. Thus, Russia has signaled that it is returning to the global stage as a major independent geopolitical player. If sustained, this move will affect the balance of power in a number of regions.

After it had disrupted the U.S.-dominated post–Cold War order during the 2014 Ukraine conflict, Russia did away with the de facto U.S. monopoly on the use of force globally. In 2015, it intervened militarily in the Syrian civil war to support the embattled government in Damascus. Many pundits scoffed at this intervention, as did the Obama administration in Washington, which confidently predicted "a quagmire" for Russia in Syria. Yet by the end of 2016, Russia and its allies on the ground managed not only to stabilize the situation for Bashar al-Assad's regime and prevent the complete collapse of the Syrian state, but also put enough pressure on the Syrian opposition and its backers to initiate a ceasefire and a political dialogue about the future of the country. The odds are against it, but if successful, the combined deployment of Russia's military power and its diplomatic resourcefulness could not only achieve a lasting result in the Middle East, but have a global impact as well.

Moscow's direct involvement has changed the geopolitical alignment in the region. Russia formed a military coalition with Syria, Iran, Hezbollah, and Iraq, a country the United States de facto controlled for a decade following its invasion and occupation in 2003. The ongoing intra-Syrian political talks are being sponsored by the diplomatic trio of Russia, Iran, and Turkey—a NATO member state that is now de facto allied with Moscow. The venue chosen for the talks is Astana, the capital of Kazakhstan, Russia's main economic and security partner in Central Asia and an active member of the Shanghai Cooperation Organization, which brings Central Asian countries together with Russia and China and, starting in 2017, also includes India and Pakistan. Beijing itself has been consistently supporting Moscow on Syria at the United Nations Security Council.

Russia's alignment with the Shia regimes in the Syrian war did not push Moscow into the anti-Sunni camp in the Middle East. Remarkably, Russia has managed to strengthen its ties with Egypt, the largest Arab Sunni country by far, and a former key Soviet ally in the region: the relationship is now being revived. Almost from scratch, Russia has built relations with the Gulf Arab countries, which had rarely remembered its existence before. In 2016, a Qatari national wealth fund bought a stake in Rosneft, Russia's main state-run oil company, despite the U.S.-imposed sanctions. After a dramatic break of seven months in 2015–2016, Moscow maneuvered Ankara toward an even closer cooperation with Russia than before.

Russian diplomacy has also managed to negotiate a number of other seemingly unbridgeable divides in the Middle East. Russia has been able to keep reasonably close and cooperative relations with Israel and the Palestinians; Israel and Iran; Iran and Saudi Arabia (and even helped negotiate an oil production cut between them); Turkey and the Kurds; similarly, the rival governments in Tripoli and Tobruk in Libya and the various politico-sectarian factions in Lebanon. There is virtually no major player in the Middle East, Hamas and Hezbollah included, with which Moscow does not have an open line and a lively dialogue. This is stunning for a country that in its Soviet past used to take very strict ideological positions and had to retreat from the region in humiliation after the lost Afghan war and the ensuing breakup of the Soviet Union itself, leading, in short order, to the bloody conflict in Chechnya.

Introduction

Having virtually left the Middle Eastern scene at the time of the first Gulf War, Russia only reappeared there two-plus decades later. The Arab Spring, cheered by Americans and Europeans as an advent of democracy, was viewed in Moscow as a major destabilization with potentially negative consequences for Russia itself. What triggered the Russian activism was the 2011 experience in Libya. There, Russia was willing in the name of partnership with the West not to block the UN Security Council's imposition of a no-fly zone to protect civilians. The UN mandate was immediately used by NATO countries to destroy the regime of Muammar Qaddafi alongside its leader, with the Libyan state itself being destroyed in the process. It was then that Russia stepped forward and prevented a similar fate for the Assad regime and Syria. This decision became a turning point for the Middle East.

Present-day Russia is too often compared with the Soviet Union. However, the country that reappeared on the Middle Eastern landscape after a long pause acts remarkably differently from its previous historical iteration. Today's Russia is essentially anti-revolutionary. A conservative power, it promotes no social and political change from the outside; in fact, it advocates just the opposite: stability of the existing regimes within the existing borders; internal accommodation reached on the basis of the balance of various interests: tribal, sectarian, national; and exclusion of domination by a single outside power. Rather than giving massive economic assistance and giving weapons for an ideological cause rather than cash, Moscow these days is clearly interested in making deals in the region, whether in the arms trade or in the energy sector, including nuclear, and seeks to attract investment from rich Gulf countries.

Yet Russia's policy goals are often deemed in the West to be hard to read; its decision-making process, centered on a single leader, is notionally opaque; and, to many outside observers, Moscow's actions look surprising, often baffling. In the age of highly polarized policy debate and openly biased reporting, propaganda and counter-propaganda, and fake news, a clear and evidence-based view of Russia's involvement in the Middle East and its impact on Moscow's broader foreign relations is hard to find. This short book attempts to address this deficit.

Specifically, it aims to answer the following questions:

- What is Moscow up to in the Middle East? What are its interests and the drivers behind those interests?

Introduction

- How does Russia's involvement in the various parts of the Middle East impact the situation there? Is there a Russian strategy for the region and if so, what is it? If the policy is a sum total of many moves, what is the trajectory, and what is the track record so far?
- How does Russia's recent activity in the Middle East impact the rest of the world, starting with Europe?
- What is the balance between Russia the competitor of the United States in the Middle East and Russia as a potential partner in the fight against the Islamic State and terrorism generally?

The book is divided into five chapters. Chapter 1, "History," deals with the legacy of the past, from the days of the Russian Empire advancing toward the Turkish Straits and pushing into Persia, to the Soviet Union's attempt to use radical Arab regimes as allies in the Cold War confrontation with the United States, and Moscow's pressure against U.S. allies Israel, Turkey, the Shah's Iran, and conservative regimes such as Saudi Arabia. The key question of this chapter is what Russia has learned from its rich historical experience with the Middle East, and how Moscow's policy was modified following the collapse of the communist system in the Soviet

Union. To the extent it is relevant, Moscow's experience in Afghanistan and the North Caucasus is also analyzed there with a view to distill the "lessons learned."

Chapter 2, "War," focuses on the continuing Russian military operation in Syria, which began in September 2015, and its political outcome. In many ways, both operationally and technologically, this military engagement constitutes a novel way in the employment of Russian military force—not only in comparison to the World War II Soviet operations in Europe and Asia, but crucially to the more recent engagements in Afghanistan and Chechnya. Since the Russian intervention in Syria is officially described as an anti-terrorist operation, this chapter looks into the methods and results of Russia's fight against terror. Of special importance is the coalition-building/-management aspect of Russian involvement in Syria, which is also new in Russia's recent military and diplomatic history.

Chapter 3, "Diplomacy," discusses the patterns of Russia's regional diplomacy. It highlights Moscow's method of negotiating regional divides by dealing simultaneously with countries and groups that are at loggerheads with one another, and promoting Russian interests with each partner. The chapter will also address the geopolitical competition and diplomatic cooperation between Russia and Turkey; Russia and the United States; and between Russia and the countries of the European Union. This chapter, structured as a series of mini-case studies, will provide an insight into the goals, strategy, and tactics of contemporary Russia as a significant outside player in the Middle East.

Chapter 4, "Trade," focuses on Russia's economic interests in the Middle East: from arms trade to hydrocarbons, nuclear energy, pipelines, and transportation infrastructure. These specific interests impact Russian decision making as much as geopolitics. In the post-2014 environment of economic restrictions imposed on Russia by the West as consequence for its actions in Ukraine, these links have assumed added importance. The chapter also addresses human relations and the ties that link Russia to the region, from the spiritual importance of the Holy Land for newly traditionalist Russia to the Russian-speaking diaspora in Israel to Russian vacationers to the impact of the Arab world on the Muslim population of Russia itself.

In the final chapter, "Conclusions," the book puts Moscow's policies in the Middle East into the broader context of its foreign policy and relations with the United States and, to a lesser extent, Europe. It begins by describing the Russian "take-away" from U.S. and Western policies, from the U.S. invasion of Iraq to the Arab Spring and the Western involvement in Libya and Syria. It then proceeds to discuss Russia's cooperation with China and India, the significance of the "Greater Eurasia" concept for Moscow's practical foreign policy, and the likely role of the Shanghai Cooperation Organization. The central question addressed here is how Moscow, through its actions in the Middle East, is seeking to change the global order, essentially from a U.S. hegemony to an oligarchy that includes Russia. The story of Russia in the Middle East is thus not only about Russia, or the Middle East.

1

History

Russia's links to the Eastern Mediterranean go back a millennium. Mediaeval Kievan princes from the tenth century occasionally raided Constantinople, but they also received Christianity there in 988. In political, religious, and cultural terms, Byzantium was the first model for Russia. Soon after the Eastern Roman Empire had been overrun by the Turks in 1453, Moscow's Grand Duke Ivan III married the niece of the last Greek emperor and adopted the Byzantine double-headed eagle as Russia's coat of arms, which is still there. From the sixteenth century, Moscow began to imagine itself as the political and spiritual heir to Constantinople, a "Third Rome," another continuing legacy. With contemporary Russia becoming increasingly conscious of its historical roots, this kind of legacy is part of the context for current policy making.

Russia Pushes South

Modern Russia's foreign policy was guided by the need to gain access to the sea, in the south as well as in the north. Just before he pushed against the Swedes in the Baltic, young Peter I, in 1695–96, engaged the Ottomans in the Black Sea area. Initially, he even thought of establishing Russia's new capital in Taganrog on the Sea of Azov, but eventually he founded St. Petersburg on the Neva, which he made Russia's capital. Peter led his troops to Bessarabia, where he was defeated, and to Persia's Caspian coast, which Russia then held for a decade.

Peter's heirs continued his work of pushing forth the borders of the empire. Catherine II annexed Crimea (1783) and the entire northern coast of the Black Sea, where she founded Odessa, a southern version of St. Petersburg. She was the first to send the Russian navy into the Mediterranean, which defeated the Ottomans in the Battle of Chesma, near Hios. She even envisaged a "Greek project," which aimed at dislodging the Turks from the Straits and creating an Orthodox empire, as a Russian dependency under her grandson, the future Alexander I, whose name was chosen with a purpose. Alexander was never crowned in Constantinople, but he helped the Greeks to achieve independence from

Turkey, and he annexed Bessarabia and much of South Caucasus.

The Persian Empire also had to give way, under Russian pressure, both in the Caucasus and the Caspian. Iran's representative at the 1919 Paris peace conference complained that imperial Russia had annexed nearly half of the former Persian possessions, including the territories of modern Azerbaijan, Armenia, and the Russian Republic of Dagestan.[1] Georgia was added to the empire, more or less peacefully, in the early nineteenth century, followed by the long and bloody conquest of the North Caucasus, only completed by 1864. In 1878, Russia pushed its borders as far as Kars in north-eastern Anatolia. Armenians under the Ottoman rule looked to it for support and protection.

It was under the 1774 Kucuk-Kaynarca treaty that Russian emperors won the right to be the protector of the Christian Orthodox population of the Ottoman Empire. Two and a half centuries before, French kings had won a similar right over all Christians. In both cases, protection of fellow Christians masked imperial designs. Eventually this led to conflict between the two powers. The formal pretext that sparked the Crimean War (1853–1856) was a dispute over the keys to the Nativity church in Bethlehem, in which Nicholas I of Russia contested the right of the French emperor Napoleon III to function as the champion of all followers of Christ in the Holy Land. With the Ottoman power progressively on the wane, Russia and major European countries began to fight over its inheritance.

The Great Game between the Russian and British Empires, which lasted the entire nineteenth century, became the epitome of Great Power rivalry across the entire continent of Eurasia. It extended from the Black Sea and the Caucasus across the Caspian and all the way to Central Asia, India, Tibet, China, and Korea. This competition resulted, among other things, in Russia expanding its rule to Turkestan, with Afghanistan becoming a buffer state between the Russian and British possessions. The mega-contest was formally declared over only in 1907, when St. Petersburg and London divided Persia into spheres of influence, with Russia getting the northern part of the country, including Tehran. This agreement also paved the way to the future alliance between Russia and Britain in the First World War.

Russia's entry into that war was motivated in no small measure by its leaders' long-standing desire to "solve the Eastern Question." That was code for taking control of the Bosporus and the Dardanelles. If successful, Russia would have secured a direct and unimpeded access to the Mediterranean, while at the same time blocking southern maritime approaches to its own heartland to any foreign competitor. During World War I, with Ottoman Turkey joining the Central Powers, Russian forces were pushing back the Turks in eastern Anatolia and also occupied neutral Persia's northwestern provinces.

Imperial Russia was mainly interested in the Straits, the Balkans, and to some extent Persia. The Arab-populated lands of the Ottoman Empire lay just outside the limit of St. Petersburg's geopolitical ambitions. The one salient exception was the Holy Land. In 1882, a Russian Imperial Palestinian Society was formed, which sponsored Russian spiritual presence in Palestine and the Levant by helping Russian pilgrims with logistics, supporting Oriental Studies, and promoting cultural links, such as by running schools, which numbered about 100 by 1914. A number of Russian churches and monasteries sprang up. St. Sergius convent house, a major complex of buildings in the heart of Jerusalem that Russia won back in the 2000s, is a massive monument to that effort. Interestingly, the society did not stop functioning after the Russian revolution and was given a major boost after 1991.

In 1915, St. Petersburg, London, and Paris secretly agreed that the Straits, Constantinople, southwestern Armenian lands, and part of northern Kurdistan would come under Russia's control, while Britain would get territories of modern Jordan, Iraq, Kuwait, and the Haifa region, and France would receive southwestern Anatolia, northern Iraq, Syria, and Lebanon. Even though the name of the Sykes-Picot agreement gives the impression that it was a purely Anglo-French deal, Russia's foreign minister Sergei Sazonov was very much involved in carving up the Ottoman Empire.

Between the World Wars

The Bolshevik revolution of 1917 was meant to be a radical break with the past ideas and practices of Russia's foreign policy. Soviet Russia renounced the treaties and agreements made by the czars. Lenin and other Soviet leaders called on the "Muslim toilers of the East" to join in the fight against imperialist colonial oppressors. Comintern, which for a time functioned as a parallel foreign ministry in Moscow, began supporting communist parties in the Middle East in their work to undermine the European colonial rule. However, the Russian Empire itself, which disintegrated in the wake of the revolution, was succeeded within five years by the Union of Soviet

Socialist Republics; this included, mainly thanks to the victorious Red Army, Armenia, Azerbaijan, Georgia, and Central Asia.

The Soviets welcomed Kemal Ataturk's Turkish Republic, made a treaty with it in 1921, and even supplied arms to Ankara. To Moscow, a Turkey that was independent from Western powers was a valuable geopolitical buffer in the Black Sea and the Caucasus region. The treaty signed in the same year between the Soviet government and Iran again provided for possible Russian reoccupation of that country: another potential buffer. With the advent of World War II, and amid fears of the Shah siding with Germany, this clause was invoked. The 1943 Tehran conference of Stalin, Roosevelt, and Churchill was held in a territory secured by the Red Army.

The war over, the Soviet forces were slow to leave Iran. Stalin had hoped that Iranian Azerbaijan, with its Soviet-inspired and -supported "people's republics," could separate from Tehran and eventually join the Soviet Union. These machinations produced the first post-World War II crisis between the USSR and its Anglo-American allies. Eventually, Stalin relented and in 1946 ordered his troops home, after which the republics were quickly snuffed out by the Shah.

In the final weeks of World War II, Stalin demanded that Turkey, which had been leaning toward Nazi Germany during the war, give the USSR special privileges in the Straits. In particular, Stalin wanted a revision of the 1936 Montreux convention, to make the Soviet Union, alongside Turkey, co-responsible for the control of the Straits. Stalin also claimed the right to build air and naval bases on the Bosporus and the Dardanelles. This demand enraged Ataturk's heirs and helped throw Ankara into Washington's arms. In 1952, Turkey acceded to NATO: a major coup for the West in the Cold War.

Having secured the Balkans for the Soviet sphere of influence as a result of World War II, Stalin also supported the Greek communists in a civil war that pitted pro-Soviet forces in the country against pro-British ones in 1944–1947. Eventually, Stalin had to give up and abandoned his allies. However, Britain's inability to sustain control over Greece led to its outreach for help to the United States. President Harry S. Truman's agreement, in 1947, to assume responsibility for keeping Greece and Turkey away from local Communists and the Soviet Union marked the beginning of the four-decade Cold War. Like Turkey, Greece joined NATO in 1952.

History

The Soviet Union Enters the Middle East

It was at that time that the Soviet Union made its first step into the geopolitics of the Middle East. Moscow became a very strong supporter of the partition of Palestine and the creation of Israel. In 1948, the Soviet Union immediately recognized the Jewish state. Stalin's aim was to undermine the British Empire, which still exercised de facto control over a number of nominally independent Arab countries. He also hoped that Israel would "build socialism" in the Holy Land. During the Arab-Israeli war of 1948–1949, the USSR trained Israeli officers and supplied arms to Israel via Czechoslovakia. Ironically, a few years later this route would be used again, this time to support Egypt vis-à-vis Israel. Having won its first war, however, Israel turned out to be a disappointment for Moscow, refusing to serve as a pro-Soviet agent in the Cold War. This led to a brief suspension of diplomatic relations between the two countries in 1952–1953, which helped provoke a fierce anti-Jewish campaign in the Soviet Union, cut short only by Stalin's death in 1953.

By that time, Moscow had switched sides, hoping to use new opportunities offered by the advent of Arab nationalism and socialism. In 1952, a military coup in Egypt toppled the pro-Western monarchy, which was the linchpin of remaining British influence in the Middle East. The coup leader Gamal Abdel Nasser moved to nationalize the Suez Canal, which turned Britain and France against Egypt. Nasser started to look for supporters in the coming clash with the major European powers, allied to the United States. In 1955, he received the first shipment of Soviet and Czechoslovak arms. This event marked the Soviet Union's first major entry into the Arab world, which soon turned it into a major player in the Middle East. Over the next three decades, the Soviet Union would send a total of 80,000 military advisers, technicians, and troops to the region, and train 55,000 Arab officers in the USSR.[2]

In 1956, as Britain, France, and Israel intervened militarily to take back control over the Suez Canal, the Soviet Union warned that it would use "missile systems" to "crush the aggressor and restore peace in the Middle East." Soviet leader Nikita Khrushchev, then busy dealing with the revolt in Hungary, did not yet have nuclear missiles ready to launch against Britain and France, but his "psychological attack"—even though the word "nuclear" was never used—worked.[3] With U.S. president Dwight Eisenhower also pressing his NATO allies to step back, the three invaders quickly retreated and Egypt triumphed. However, after 1956 the Middle East became a major battlefield of Soviet-American rivalry in the Cold War.

The Soviet Union hoped to capitalize on the political revolutions in the Middle East. As nationalists, inspired by quasi-socialist ideas as much as by Nasser's example, toppled pro-Western regimes in a number of other Arab countries, such as Iraq (1958, 1963), and Northern Yemen (1962), they all were befriended by Moscow, which offered them economic assistance, arms, and military advisers. In Northern Yemen alone, for example, in 1963 there were over 500 Soviet servicemen.[4] The USSR also supported the national liberation movements in Algeria, which succeeded in 1962 to end French rule, and in Southern Yemen, which in 1967 ended Britain's protectorate. Soviet Communist ideologues saw new Arab leaders as allies in the global contest against Western capitalism and hoped that they would be eventually swayed toward Communism.

At the same time, Moscow viewed conservative Middle Eastern regimes, along with the Shah of Iran, as both ideological and politico-military adversaries. After all, the Central Treaty Organization (CENTO), composed of Iran, Iraq (until 1958), Pakistan, Turkey, and the United Kingdom, with very close support from the United States, was part of the global system of anti-Soviet alliances in the Cold War, alongside NATO in Europe and SEATO in Southeast Asia. Turkey hosted U.S. Jupiter missiles pointed at close range toward the Soviet Union, which Khrushchev sought to counter by deploying Soviet missiles in Cuba in 1962, while Pakistan was a base for U.S. spy overflights of the USSR, one of which, in 1960, ended in the downing of the plane, the capture of its pilot, and the scuttling of the Soviet-Western summit in Paris. Of course, the regimes of Turkey, Iran, and Pakistan practiced highly repressive policies against local communists. Yet the Soviet Union did not itself plot revolutions against Arab monarchies or those it called "reactionary regimes," preferring to rely on the "forces of history" instead.

The 1967 and 1973 Arab-Israeli Wars

In the Six Day War of 1967, Moscow fully supported Egypt and Syria against Israel's attack. It immediately broke off diplomatic relations with Israel and greatly enhanced its military assistance to the Arabs. Paradoxically, even though the Arab countries supported by Moscow lost the war, Soviet influence in the region, rather than ebbing, actually grew. In 1968–1969, as Egypt and Syria moved even closer to Moscow, left-leaning regimes came to power in Iraq, Sudan, and Libya, which strengthened their ties to the USSR.

In Egypt, the Soviet Navy received the right to use several ports (Alexandria, Port Said, and Marsa Matrouh), which allowed the USSR to keep a Mediterranean squadron (established in July 1967) permanently in the area. The Soviet Air Force won the right to use Egyptian airfields. In 1970, the Soviet Union covertly deployed—as part of "Operation Caucasus"—a whole air defense division (over 11,000 men) and an air brigade in the Suez Canal zone to stop Israeli attacks on Egyptian planes. It worked: Israel suffered losses and had to agree to a formal cease-fire. By attracting heavy Soviet military presence (15,000–20,000 men) in Egypt, Nasser sought to make sure that the Soviet Union was immediately drawn into the next war on the side of the Arabs.[5]

Simultaneously, the Soviet Union began to support the Palestine Liberation Organization, which it recognized as the sole representative of the Palestinian people, and other Palestinian organizations, such as the "democratic" and "popular" fronts for the liberation of Palestine (known as the DFLP and PFLP). It secretly supplied them with portable anti-aircraft missiles and tanks. Some 1,500 Palestinian fighters were trained in the Soviet Union.[6] Other Warsaw Pact countries, such as East Germany, did their share of supporting militant Palestinian groups.

Soon, however, Moscow suffered a sudden and important setback in its regional contest with the United States. In July 1972, just a year after the Soviet-Egyptian treaty on friendship and cooperation was signed, Anwar Sadat, who in 1970 succeeded Nasser as president of Egypt, expelled 20,000 Soviet military advisers from the country and terminated Soviet basing rights in Egypt. At the time, this was received in Moscow as a major political blow, which it definitely was. However, this act also reduced the risk of the Soviet Union being directly drawn into a coming war in the Middle East. What Sadat had in mind was launching a war of revenge against Israel, and he did not want to be held back by Soviet advisers. He also was getting ready to switch sides in the Cold War.

In October 1973, Egypt and Syria attacked Israel—against the advice of and without consulting Moscow. Yet the Soviet Union immediately came to the Arab side and began a massive sea- and airlift to Cairo and Damascus. Soviet crews operated some of Egypt's air defenses. Three dozen Soviet ships and two dozen submarines were concentrated in the Mediterranean. When the war, after the Arabs' initial success, was rapidly turning into a disaster for them, Moscow made it clear it would not permit a military collapse of Egypt and Syria, and began preparations for sending Soviet airborne troops to the region. Washington reacted by placing its strategic nuclear forces on alert.

That upped the ante enormously. The concern at the time in the Kremlin, just as in the White House, was that a regional imbroglio started by one superpower's client states would escalate to the global level and risk a nuclear war between America and Russia. Eventually, U.S. secretary of state Henry Kissinger had to urgently travel to Moscow to deescalate the situation. Unlike in 1967, when the Soviet Union lost thirty-five dead in the Arab-Israeli war, in 1973 Soviet military personnel took no part in the fighting and sustained no losses.

The war that started well but ended in a major debacle for the Arabs pushed Cairo to seek peace with Israel and thus move even closer to Washington. Kissinger's shuttle diplomacy in 1973 led to a peace process that culminated in the 1978 Camp David agreement and soon thereafter establishment of diplomatic relations between Egypt and Israel. President Sadat abrogated the treaty with the USSR and suspended repayment of debts to Moscow.

The Soviet Union "lost" Egypt, which made it to the U.S. camp, and Sadat was described by Soviet propaganda as a U.S. stooge.

Soviet positions in the Middle East suffered. Only Damascus, Tripoli, and the PLO rejected reconciliation with the enemy and formed a "rejection front" supported by Moscow. It was then that Syria became the Soviet Union's closest ally in the region. No longer welcome at Egyptian ports, the 5th Mediterranean Squadron of the Soviet Navy started to use Syria's Tartus as a supply and maintenance facility. Yet Syrian president Hafez al-Assad was a tough partner, using the Soviets much more than allowing them to use him. Others, from Algeria to South Yemen, continued to receive Soviet arms and only nominally follow the Soviet lead in world politics. The oil-rich nations of Iraq and Libya, with headstrong leaders Saddam Hussein and Muammar Qaddafi, pursued stridently independent policies while buying Soviet weapons.

The Iranian Revolution and the War in Afghanistan

The Iranian revolution of 1979, with its clear anti-American overtones, led the Soviet leaders to conclude, for the first time, that "liberation strug- gle can also be waged under the banner of Islam."[7] Geopolitically, this was undoubtedly a big and unexpected gain for Moscow, even though Soviet- Iranian relations under the shah were peaceful and generally cooperative. The Islamic revolution ended Iran's status as an ally of the United States: thou- sands of U.S. military personnel and contractors were expelled from the country, and U.S. military intelligence facilities closed. America became, to the new Iranian authorities, the "Great Satan."

Ayatollah Khomeini, however, did not switch sides in the Cold War, like Sadat before him. Iranian revolutionaries did not spare the USSR, which they branded the "Little Satan." Communists and other leftists with Moscow connections were crushed and persecuted early on. Khomeini and his fol- lowers looked at the Soviet Union first of all as an atheist country that lorded over millions of Muslims. Moscow began to fear Tehran's attempts at exporting the ideas of Islamic revolution to the southern republics of the Soviet Union, particularly Azerbaijan, where most people were traditionally Shia.

Enthused by the massive blow to the U.S. posi- tion in the Middle East as a consequence of the Iranian revolution, the Soviet leadership committed a major blunder of its own by intervening militarily in Afghanistan, a neighboring country where local pro-Communist elements had seized power but soon fell out among themselves and were in danger of losing to forces opposed to radical transformation of a deeply traditionalist society. The logic of the Cold War did not allow either superpower to let a friendly regime succumb to an internal crisis that would be immediately exploited by the competitor. Moscow walked into a trap.

The ten-year Soviet war in Afghanistan (1979–1989) left behind a huge trauma but also endowed Moscow with precious experience. It resulted in 14,000 Soviet servicemen—and about an estimated million Afghans—dead, spread malaise in Soviet society, and contributed massively to a reorientation of Soviet foreign policy by Mikhail Gorbachev. At the same time, Russians learned to appreciate the resilience of Muslim guerillas, the vitality and consolidating power of Islam, and the intricacies of traditional societies. The "Afghan syndrome" commanded Moscow to never again seek to impose one's ideology and one's rule on a Muslim country.

The Afghan War for the first time demonstrated to Moscow the strength of Islamist radicalism and the power of cross-border Muslim solidarity. It also taught it to regard alliances and alignments in that part of the world as essentially tactical and easily shifting, with no permanent friends and no eternal enemies. That experience would come in handy soon, as the Soviet Union began to unravel just thirty months after the withdrawal of Soviet military forces from Afghanistan. In Tajikistan and then in the North Caucasus, Russia confronted an enemy that bore close resemblance to the Afghan mujahedeen.

In the Middle East itself, in the war between Iran and Iraq (1980–1988), which ran concurrently with the Soviet intervention in Afghanistan, Moscow, after initial hesitation, continued to send arms to Baghdad, even though it was the Iraqi dictator Saddam Hussein who started the war—without prior consultations with Moscow and after having exterminated potential local rivals, including communists. Like so many Arab clients of Moscow, he was wary of the Soviet Union's desire to spread communism. During the war, Hussein moved closer to the United States, in order to capitalize on Washington's hostility toward the Iranian Islamist revolutionaries. Despite the existence of a Treaty of Friendship between Iraq and the USSR, signed in 1972, Baghdad's ties to Moscow were visibly fraying.

Through the 1980s, the Middle East remained

very much a Cold War battlefield. The Saudis were most actively supporting the Afghan resistance to the Soviet forces and the regime in Kabul that Moscow had installed. In 1986, the Saudis, in coordination with the Americans, engineered a steep plunge in oil prices that undermined Soviet hard currency revenues and led to the financial crisis that contributed massively to the erosion of the Soviet empire and eventually the downfall of the Soviet Union.

The Soviet Union's friends in the Middle East also came under attack. In 1982, Israel succeeded in driving the PLO out of Lebanon. During that war, Moscow sent an air defense brigade—around 8,000 soldiers—to protect Syria against Israeli strikes. The troops were withdrawn in 1984.[8] In 1986 the U.S. Air Force bombed Libya in retaliation for the Libyan role in a Berlin restaurant bombing plot. In the same year, pro-Soviet South Yemen, where the USSR built a naval facility for its Indian Ocean squadron, fell to a coup d'etat and was plunged into chaos. Bogged down in Afghanistan and facing unrest in Poland, Moscow was unable to protect its regional allies and friends.

With Egypt's *volte face* in 1973, Moscow lost its most important stronghold in the Arab world. Since then, the Soviet Union never regained the momentum it had from the mid-1950s through the early

1970s. The Soviet drive in the region ran out of steam, and Moscow's positions began to decline. The war in Afghanistan was particularly damaging to the Soviet standing in the Arab and more broadly the Muslim world. Not only the Pakistanis and the Saudis, but the Egyptians, Iranians, and Turks were part of a coalition that made the Soviet Union consent in 1988 to withdraw its forces from Afghanistan. The pullout was completed by February 1989.

The Gulf War and the Soviet Union's Demise

The Soviet political retreat from the Middle East followed in short order. As with his attack on Iran in 1980, Iraq's Saddam Hussein surprised Moscow again in August 1990 with his invasion of Kuwait. Immediately, the Kremlin joined the White House in strongly condemning Iraqi aggression and attempted annexation of a sovereign country. In the new spirit of Soviet-American rapprochement, it may have appeared to some as a welcome sign of cooperation between the two powers instead of their former bitter confrontation. The reality was more nuanced.

Essentially, the United States emerged as the

only world power capable of decisive action in the region. The Soviet Union's role was reduced to being America's follower. When Soviet president Mikhail Gorbachev, through Evgeny Primakov, Moscow's leading Arabist,[9] tried to pursue his own line in the Kuwait crisis by reaching out to Saddam to get him to agree to give up Kuwait without a fight, not only did he fail in his effort in Baghdad, but he was double-crossed in Washington. The George H.W. Bush administration was determined to teach Saddam a lesson and inaugurate a new world order in which there was only one superpower. Moscow's mediation was unwelcome and went nowhere. This was, to all practical purposes, the end of the Soviet Union's role in the Middle East.

True, the USSR until virtually the last weeks of its existence was trying to adjust to the dramatically changing environment. Very late in the game, in the fall of 1991, Gorbachev finally went ahead to restore diplomatic relations with Israel. The first Soviet ambassador after the long break in relations arrived in Israel as the USSR envoy, only to present his credentials as the ambassador of the Russian Federation. In November 1991, the Soviet Union played the part of a formal co-chair of the Arab-Israeli peace conference in Madrid, but it was clear to everyone that Moscow was there as an add-on:

it was Washington that was ruling supreme, from now on.

The Russian Federation's Low Profile

The breakup of the Soviet Union in 1991 physically separated Russia from the Middle East due to the emergence of several independent states in place of the former Soviet republics of Armenia, Azerbaijan, and Georgia in the Caucasus, and Kazakhstan, Kyrgyzstan, Tajikistan, Turkmenistan, and Uzbekistan in Central Asia. The collapse of the unified Soviet state immediately led to conflicts in a number of new entities, drawing Russia in politically and in some cases militarily. In Tajikistan, Russian forces became embroiled in a civil war; in Georgia, they intervened in ethnic conflicts in Abkhazia and South Ossetia.

In the 1990s, Russia was nearly totally consumed by its own post-Communist transformation, the consequences of the collapse of the Soviet Union, and the bloody conflict in Chechnya. Moscow de facto withdrew from the wider world, limiting its horizon to the former Soviet Union and focusing on its relations with the West, on which the Russian Federation was now dependent financially, economically, and politically. The new Russian leadership cut off the life line to the Najibullah regime in Kabul, which had managed to hold out for two and a half years even without Soviet troops. This allowed the mujahedeen to take over in 1992. The Middle East almost vanished from the suddenly shrunken world of Russian foreign policy.

However, some contacts with the region persisted and some novel developments were afoot. Above all, this related to Turkey. Economic ties between Russia and Turkey expanded due to the very active shuttle trade operated by ordinary Russians and the very robust expansion of the Turkish construction industry into the Russian market. Those Russians who have first managed to profit from transition to a market economy quickly discovered the beaches of Antalya and other Turkish Mediterranean resorts. These people-to-people contacts were changing the very fabric of the Russo-Turkish relations.

Surely, the legacy of wars and decades of more recent hostility during the Cold War were all there. Western-orientated Turkish elites continued to look at Russia with suspicion. Moscow's alliance with Armenia, locked in a bitter conflict with pro-Turkish Azerbaijan over Nagorno-Karabakh, weighed in on the relationship. Russians, for their part, could not ignore the support the Circassian diaspora in

Turkey was giving to Chechen rebels in the North Caucasus, and the role the Turkish intelligence services were playing there. Moscow was also concerned by pan-Turkic ambitions of then president Turgut Ozal, who was promoting special relations with the Turkic-speaking former Soviet republics of Central Asia and Azerbaijan. Yet the overall balance in Russo-Turkish relations was decidedly positive.

Relations with Iran also warmed up, following the end of the Soviet Union. More than a decade after the founding of the Islamic republic, the revolutionary fervor in Tehran had calmed down. There was no question of exporting Islamism to the former Soviet borderlands. Just the opposite: Iranian leaders became concerned about the potential of instability on its own northern border, no longer controlled from Moscow. Cooperation rather than competition was in order. In 1997, Russia and Iran managed to broker a peace deal that ended a five-year civil war in Tajikistan, the only Farsi-speaking ex-republic of the USSR, and the only post-Soviet conflict that was actually put to rest in the quarter-century since the demise of the Soviet Union.

Iranians also took a pragmatic stance on the issue of Chechnya. Rather than supporting the rebels or expressing sympathy with them, they saw the conflict in geopolitical terms, fearing even more instability in the Caucasus. While in the chair of the Islamic Conference Organization, Tehran promoted Russia's observer status within the organization. Russians, for their part, did not share the Western view of Iran as a state sponsor of terrorism. With the triumph of the Taliban in Afghanistan in 1996, Iran and Russia found themselves on the same side, opposing the new extremist rulers of the country. In sum, Moscow saw Iran as a major regional power in a difficult setting, seeking ways to bolster its position vis-à-vis its Arab and Turkish neighbors, while in a long-term confrontation with the United States and Israel.

Russia began to develop business projects with Iran, in particular in the nuclear energy field. Rosatom took over the construction of the Bushehr nuclear power plant from the German company Siemens. Russia also began arms shipments to Iran. Yet Moscow took a dim view of Iran's nuclear and missile programs. Russia was successor to the Soviet Union also in terms of its guardianship of the non-proliferation of weapons of mass destruction (WMD). A rare public report by the Russian Foreign Intelligence Service (SVR) in 1993 focused on the risks of Iran's missile development program.[10] Russian counter-intelligence thwarted Iranian attempts to get hold of Russian nuclear and missile secrets, and to recruit Russian engineers and scientists. Yet, as with Turkey, the positives clearly outweighed the negatives.

9/11 and the U.S. Invasion of Iraq

When Al Qaeda terrorists attacked New York and Washington on September 11, 2011, Vladimir Putin immediately called George W. Bush and offered Russia's support. This was a major strategic move. Never before had Moscow aligned with Washington in the Middle East so closely and so unambiguously. Putin, who had been prosecuting his own war on terror in the North Caucasus, hoped to get the United States as an ally in that fight. Russia went beyond verbal support and symbolic actions, such as postponing a strategic forces exercise, to give real political and intelligence support to the U.S. military operation in Afghanistan. Russia's partners in the anti-Taliban Northern Alliance provided most of the ground forces in the U.S.-led operation.

Yet Moscow's hope of building an alliance with the United States and NATO based on a joint fight against international terrorism was soon dispelled. The Bush administration did not see much value in a closer relationship with Russia, widely seen as a power in terminal decline. Washington refused to count Chechnya as a battlefield in the fight against terrorism and began to focus on Iraq, which, under Saddam, remained "unfinished business" from the time of the first President Bush.

In Iraq, Russia, while supportive of the UN Security Council resolutions adopted after the invasion of Kuwait, protested against the liberal use of force by the United States and Britain without special authorization by the Security Council. Moscow supported the work of international inspectors monitoring Iraqi activities in the WMD field, but it was unhappy that the inspector teams were often led by people too close to Washington. As in the run-up to the First Gulf War, Moscow tried to mediate between Baghdad, with which it still had important business ties, and Washington.

It failed again. After 9/11, there was no stopping the Bush administration from attacking Iraq. At the UN Security Council, Russia, alongside France and China, refused to allow the use of force against Iraq. In March 2003, however, the United States, followed by Britain, invaded regardless. The budding partnership between Moscow and Washington, which had emerged in the wake of 9/11, became irrevocably fractured. To Moscow, this was another powerful argument—after the NATO bombing of

Yugoslavia in 1999—to treat the United States as a dangerous nation. Subsequently, Russia joined with other countries to put the Iraq situation under some sort of UN monitoring, and eventually accepted the new authorities in Baghdad, but it never accepted the U.S. "aggression."

To Russian officials, the U.S. invasion of Iraq in 2003 has been the prime source of the current turmoil in the Arab world. Not only was it undertaken for the wrong reasons: Iraq was revealed to have had no active WMD program, and Saddam Hussein was not cooperating with Al Qaeda. Not only did it fail to reach its stated objectives, "draining the swamp" where terrorists are bred and building a functioning democracy in Iraq. It destroyed a key secular state between the Gulf and the Levant, and let loose sectarianism, radicalism, and terrorism, which mutated to the new form of an "Islamic state." The end of Saddam's brutal dictatorship, in the Russian analysis, was not enough to compensate for that.

The Arab Spring

Seen from Moscow, the Arab Spring that began in late 2010 in Tunisia was the result of a combination of sociopolitical and demographic processes in the

Arab world, in the broader context of globaliza-
tion.[11] Too many young men found their aspirations
for decent living standards thwarted by the cor-
rupt and complacent political systems in place in
their countries. In contrast to this scholarly view,
senior Russian officials focused on the support and
encouragement that Arab "spring revolutionaries"
began to receive from Western governments and
societies.[12] To the Kremlin, this was part of a general strategy to promote Western-style democracy
in the Middle East and replace the increasingly
incompetent and vulnerable regimes, many of them
pro-Western, with ones which would be both pro-
Western and democratically legitimate, and thus
consolidate and even increase U.S. and European
influence in the region.

Taken in a global context, the Arab Spring was
believed by the Moscow officialdom to be a con-
tinuation of "color revolutions," a series of events
that began in 2000 in Belgrade, where Slobodan
Milosevic was toppled by street protesters, and
went on to change governments, using more or less
the same techniques, in Georgia (2003), Ukraine
(2004–2005), and Kyrgyzstan (2005). Kremlin
leaders were worried that, since conditions broadly
similar to those prevailing in the Middle East were
also present in the former Soviet republics of Central

Asia and in Russia's own North Caucasus, a large swath of Russia's neighborhood, from the Black Sea to the Caspian and the Urals to the Chinese border, might get restless, abetted by foreign instigation. Sparks from Arab revolutions could ignite Russia's geopolitical "underbelly."

What is more, the new Western enthusiasm for promoting democracy in regions that had been regarded as strongholds of authoritarianism led to suspicions in and around the Kremlin that Western and Western-funded Russian NGOs might try to bring about a "Russian spring." These suspicions appeared vindicated by the wave of mass protests that suddenly rose in Moscow in the winter of 2011–2012 and challenged Putin personally more than anything since his coming to power in 2000. The Kremlin stood firm, employing a strategy of token concessions and targeted repression, and the protests soon fizzled out. However, the Kiev Maidan of 2013–2014 gave them a sense of what a successful urban revolt might look like, and what consequences it could lead to. This in turn strength-ened Moscow's resolve to oppose destabilizing trends in the Middle East.

Domestic concerns definitely colored Moscow's response to the Arab Spring, but this was not the whole story. Russian experts in the region from the start were skeptical that upheavals in Arab countries would actually lead to democratic transformation as hoped for in the West. In the Russian analysis, Islamism was a far more likely beneficiary: "Islamist winter" was the next station after the aborted democratic spring. These experts feared less a reassertion of U.S. regional influence by means of democratic, as opposed to military, regime change than Washington's loss of control of the developments and the ensuing fast-spreading chaos that would engulf the region and empower the most extreme forces in the Arab world. To Russian Arabists, Americans and their European allies were no more than hapless sorcerer's apprentices who did not know what they were doing.

The idea that the Arab Spring was a U.S. plot is clearly preposterous, no matter how big a role the social media or foreign-funded NGOs played in the overthrow of President Hosni Mubarak in Egypt. Conspiracy theories, popular with some Russians, which claim that the United States had a secret strategy to strengthen its dominance by fomenting chaos that Washington would be able to steer in a direction that favored its interests, hold no water. Over time, America the Almighty was transformed, in the eyes of the Russian state-run media, into an America that had lost control and became driven by events.

The Kremlin itself took a pragmatic stance. It had dealt with Islamists in power before, whether in Turkey, where the Justice and Development (AKP) party assumed power in 2002, or in Gaza, controlled by Hamas. Even before Egypt's 2012 democratic elections gave victory to the Muslim Brotherhood's candidate, Russian representatives had established contact with them. Newly elected president Mohammed Morsi was soon invited to travel to Russia for talks with Vladimir Putin. Yet a year later Moscow was relieved to see the Egyptian military take over and stop what looked like a quickening slide toward chaos in the Arab world's largest country. The Arab Spring was over.

The Libyan Crisis

In early 2011, Russians watched in amazement as the United States first pulled the plug on their Egyptian ally, Hosni Mubarak, after a week of mass protests in Cairo's Tahrir Square, and then put up with Muslim Brotherhood Islamists in power. It was in Libya, however, that the Russians became active themselves. The crisis in Libya taught Moscow an important lesson that determined not only its attitude to the developments in the Middle East, but also its general approach to relations with the United States and its judgment on the European Union.

When the uprising in Libya started in February 2011, Russia was formally led by President Dmitry Medvedev, but in reality it was still very much controlled by Vladimir Putin, in his role as prime minister. Medvedev, Putin's protégé, was given a brief from his mentor to try to form a comprehensive partnership with the West: political, economic, and military. As it turned out, this was the last such attempt in Russia's post-Soviet history, after Boris Yeltsin's in the early 1990s and Putin's own a decade later. And it ended in utter failure, effectively foreclosing that route for the future.

In Libya, after it had written off Qaddafi's debt to the late USSR in 2008, Moscow had several contracts for arms and infrastructure projects totaling some $7 billion. It certainly wanted to keep those. On the other hand, Moscow had no special political ties to Muammar Qaddafi and his regime. Libya was on the far periphery of Russian geopolitical interests. Thus, Moscow let Libya be a test case of its relations with the United States and Europe. Russia hoped to partner with the West in Libya to help manage the internal conflict, save civilian lives, and work toward a new constitution for the

country. It expected, however, that such cooperation would be organized on an equal basis, under
the UN Security Council auspices, and would take
account of Russia's material interests in Libya.

In that spirit, Russia for the first time did not
block a Security Council resolution installing a
no-fly zone in Libya to prevent a feared massacre
in Benghazi as Qaddafi was mounting a counter-
offensive against his opponents. In reality, the use
of force by NATO against Qaddafi's forces resulted
in a regime change, the killing of the dictator, and
the complete disintegration of the Libyan state.
Qaddafi's vast arsenals were looted, and weapons
from there found their way to various parts of the
Middle East and Africa. Libya, by now a geographi-
cal concept only, became one of the strongholds
of Islamist extremists. The Russian contracts, of
course, were lost.

Even as the conflict in Libya was still in progress
and its outcome, after a sluggish NATO start, was
unclear, Putin voiced concerns about the Western-
led operation that had become possible as a result
of Moscow's Security Council abstention. Rather
than a spat between Putin and Medvedev, who was
publicly highly critical of Qaddafi and strongly
supportive of the rapprochement with the West,
this was more likely part of a reassurance policy

that Moscow had embarked upon. This policy was best illustrated by Moscow sending envoys both to the revolutionary headquarters in Benghazi and Qaddafi's court in Tripoli.

The conclusions that Moscow eventually drew from its engagement in Libya could be summarized as the West is not to be trusted—once they pocket your concession, they ignore you; the United States and its allies have no compunctions about going beyond the limits set by UN resolutions; Americans and Europeans are guided by grand but faulty ideologies *and* petty interests, as they lack strategic vision and fail to foresee even the immediate consequences of their actions. Thus, going forward the Libya experience would not be repeated in Russia's foreign policy. These conclusions had an immediate effect in Syria, where an uprising against the Assad regime started in March 2011.

The Syrian Crisis

By the spring of 2011, Syria was not Moscow's ally the way it was in the Cold War decades. Bashar al-Assad had visited Moscow only once, to get the debt his father owed to the Soviet Union written off. As Putin later quipped, the Syrian president was spending more time in Paris and London than in Moscow.[13] Tartus had degraded to a dilapidated facility with a staff of fifty. In terms of arms trade, Syria was not among Russia's most important customers. Overall two-way trade was negligible. However, it was in Syria that Putin decided to make a point that U.S.-driven regime change in the Middle East had limits; that outside military intervention in Syria would not be permitted; and that the world's supreme authority, in matters of war and peace, was the UN Security Council, where Russia had veto power. Moscow's position on Syria was not so much about Syria or even the Middle East; it was about the global order.

Not that the Kremlin and Russian diplomats and intelligence officers on the ground in Syria did not see the heavy-handedness of the Syrian regime. In 2011 and later, Russian diplomats counseled the Baath authorities to make concessions to the opposition. These suggestions, however, were ignored in Damascus. Assad probably realized that Russia would protect his regime anyway. He was not wholly wrong. With the experience of Libya still very fresh and Putin back in the Kremlin from May 2012, Russia's approach to relations with the West toughened. At the UN Security Council, Russia began blocking any draft resolution that might have constituted a pretext for foreign military intervention in Syria. At the same time, Russia began supplying the Assad regime with the arms he needed to put down the domestic revolt. Syria was meant to be the place where the momentum of the Arab Spring and Libya-style intervention would be stopped.

Russian analysts advised the Kremlin that Assad, for all the flaws and failings of his regime, had a fairly good chance of surviving the domestic storm, if given protection from outside interference. This was in stark contrast to U.S. government experts on whose advice President Barack Obama famously said that Bashar al-Assad would not last long.[14] With the U.S.-Russian "reset" on hold, due to the U.S. election campaign, but not yet terminated, this disagreement in analysis was not yet an obstacle to attempts at cooperation between Moscow and Washington.

In June 2012, the United States and Russia brokered a joint statement in Geneva that foresaw negotiations between the Syrian government and the opposition and the creation of a transitional authority. Moscow, which cared about its wider global and regional goals much more than about the personality of Bashar al-Assad, was ready to work on a political solution but unwilling to drop Assad as a precondition. The Obama administration saw things differently. Its aim was an early replacement of Assad and his regime. This would have been a victory for democracy, as well as a geopolitical win over Iran, which had turned Damascus into an ally on Israel's border. The Geneva Communique fell flat virtually the day after its adoption.

With Obama winning a second term and Assad still in power in Damascus, the Kremlin was ready for a fresh attempt at political settlement. When U.S. secretary of state John Kerry visited Moscow in May 2013, Putin suggested to him that Russia and the United States jointly steer Syria toward peace, by applying pressure on the parties closest to them and closely coordinating between themselves, a sort of a "Dayton *à deux*," in reference to the accords that ended the Balkan crisis in the 1990s. Americans, however, never bought the analogy. What they needed was Russia's cooperation in dislodging Assad, for a fee, such as U.S. consent to Russia keeping its facility in Tartus and continuing to supply arms to the new Syrian regime. Over the summer it became increasingly clear there was not going to be a deal.

In August 2013, following a chemical attack in Ghoutta near Damascus, which the United States blamed on the Syrian government, Washington began considering a military strike against Syria as punishment for the use of chemical weapons.

President Obama was highly reluctant to commit the United States to another military operation in the Middle East, but he was under pressure from his political opponents and public opinion to honor his own "red line" in dealing with Assad. It was at this point that Vladimir Putin saw an opportunity, and was quick and adroit enough to exploit it.

During a brief encounter on the margins of the G20 summit in St. Petersburg in early September 2013, Putin offered Obama a deal to rid Syria of chemical weapons in exchange for the United States abstaining from attacking it. Obama, the reluctant warrior, accepted; Assad was persuaded to give up his chemical weapons arsenal, whose existence Damascus had never acknowledged; Russian and American officials and experts agreed on the parameters of the operation; other countries joined in to give it a flavor of an international community engagement. By 2014, amidst the ongoing civil war, Syrian chemical weapons had been taken out of the country and neutralized. For Moscow, this was a major coup: for the first time since the end of the Cold War, they could deal with Americans as equals.

*

This brief outline of Russia's involvement in the Middle East leads to the following conclusion. Russia is not a newcomer to the region. It has a rich history of involvement there. Traditionally, Russia was mostly looking at the region from a geopolitical perspective. Security factors played a salient role in the Russian calculus. Often, the Middle East was a playground where Russia competed against rival great powers. In the globalized, interconnected environment of the twenty-first century, the Middle East as the heart of the turbulent Muslim world has a direct bearing on developments within Russia's own sizable and growing indigenous Muslim community. Thus, Russia's global standing as a great power and its own integrity and stability depend to a significant degree on how it fares in the Middle East. In 2015, President Putin decided to intervene militarily in Syria, which involved Russia for the first time in its history in a war in the Arab world. That ongoing experience, which is discussed in the next chapter, will shape Russia's role in the region and beyond for years to come.

2

War

Russians have been active militarily on the edges of the Middle East for centuries. Against Ottoman Turkey alone, Russia waged twelve wars. It took the czarist army half a century to prevail over the mountaineers of the North Caucasus. Russia also conquered Turkestan, now Central Asia, where after the Bolshevik revolution the Red Army had to put down resistance of local "feudal lords," making its surviving fighters flee to Afghanistan. Fifty to sixty years later, some of these fighters' descendants joined the Afghan mujahedeen to turn the Soviet forces away. Right after the breakup of the Soviet Union, the Russian Federation intervened in a civil war in Tajikistan and then waged two campaigns in the North Caucasus. However, neither the Russian Empire nor the Soviet Union had ever fought directly in the Arab lands. In 2015, this changed, as Russia stepped into the Syrian conflict.

The Russian military operation in Syria is not only the biggest combat employment of Russia's armed forces abroad since the Afghan war; it represents a very different kind of warfare in comparison to anything Russia had practiced before. First, this is an expeditionary war: Russia is fighting in a country with which it has no common border. Second, this is predominantly an air war: Russian ground forces are not fighting, though the navy is occasionally engaged. Third, this is a coalition war: in order to achieve the war's aims, Russian airstrikes have to be exploited by the non-Russian forces operating on the ground. Fourth, this is a limited war very closely tied to the diplomatic process.

A War of Choice

In Syria, it was Moscow's decision to go in or to stay put. Conceivably, President Putin could have watched the Assad regime go under, the jihadis triumph, and Syria unravel, turning into another Libya. Russia would have surely suffered the consequences, but not before others, including Turkey and the European Union. Assad was an asset, as long as he was capable of doing the fighting, but hardly a close ally impossible to dump. The Middle East, one could argue, was a mess, would remain so for decades, and stepping into the fray would be courting disaster. The Afghan syndrome was still there to guard against adventurism in foreign Muslim lands. If even the United States was unable to manage the region, what were Russia's chances, particularly given the ongoing conflict in Ukraine and the deepening confrontation with the West? Wouldn't it be wiser instead to focus on one's domestic security vis-à-vis Muslim extremists and radicals and, at most, shore up Moscow's allies in Central Asia—the region it absolutely could not afford to lose to the jihadis?

This reasoning might have been on some Russian officials' minds, but not on Vladimir Putin's. Like in Crimea and Donbass Ukraine eighteen months before, he stepped forward, not back. Putin again took the initiative, guided by the maxim he learned as a boy in Leningrad, and then quoted: "If a fight is inevitable, strike first." There was a difference, however. Whereas the 2014 military action in Ukraine constituted, in the eyes of the Kremlin, strategic defense of Russia's immediate security space and a counter-punch against the trespassers, Syria was clearly an offensive, preventative move.

Putin's decision to go in rather than to hold back was in many ways similar to his September 1999 choice to cross the Terek River and move into the mountains of Chechnya to crush the terrorists rather than halt at the foothills and try to isolate the enemy. Then, and possibly also now, Putin was alone in his pro-active approach among the civilian leadership. Then, and certainly now, he was supported by the military top brass and the security chiefs. The die was cast.

Syria, to Russia, was not just another Arab country. It was a Soviet ally, and then a Russian arms client.[1] Moscow has kept a naval resupply facility in Tartus, its only installation of that kind in the Mediterranean, even though, by the 2000s, it had considerably degraded. As part of Russia's military modernization drive, the Russian navy in 2008 began planning an upgrade of the facility to a veritable naval base by 2020. Alternatives, such as Cyprus and Montenegro, turned out to be off-limits due to those countries' EU or NATO membership. No less important, Syria, since the mid-1950s, has been the center of Moscow's political influence and intelligence presence in the region. In Tel Al-Hara, Deraa province, Russia kept a listening post to monitor Israeli movements.[2] Many Syrian military officers were trained in the Soviet Union, and some had Russian wives. In the 1990s, during the Chechen war, the Syrian intelligence services cooperated with Moscow to prevent the local Circassian diaspora's support for the anti-Russian militants and terrorists.

Having decided in 2011 that "Syria would be no Libya," Moscow shipped arms to the embattled government in Damascus, to help it fight the insurgency. Russia also gave Syria diplomatic protection, vetoing a series of UN Security Council draft resolutions that might be construed as a basis for future intervention. Yet by early 2015 the Syrian government forces were clearly losing ground in places like Idlib (threatening Latakia, the prime bastion of the Alawite community), Deraa (putting Damascus at risk), and Tadmor (ancient Palmyra), visibly crumbling under pressure from the opposition coalition of Jabkhat al Nusra, Jaysh al Fateh (including Ahrar al-Sham), and Jund al-Aqsa, enjoying Saudi, Turkish, and Qatari support. Russian government analysts concluded that Assad's defeat was inevitable. That raised the prospect of the fall not just of the House of Assad, but of the Syrian state with it, and a likely triumph of Islamist radicals of the Nusra front and the Caliphate.

To Vladimir Putin, the consequences of such an outcome were too dangerous to allow it to happen.

Putin rose to the leadership of Russia as an implacable fighter against terrorists and other jihadis, ready to go all the way to do them in. In 1999, he saw the danger of the Chechen raid into Dagestan in a potential destabilization of all of Russia's Muslim regions. Then, links between North Caucasus terrorists in Russia and their brethren in the Arab world were strong and visible. A number of Arab "amirs," of field commanders, were killed by the Russian security forces in the North Caucasus. In 2015, the danger of the Islamic State and other jihadis taking over Syria extended, in Putin's eyes, to Russia's immediate Central Asian neighborhood and to Russia's own twenty-million-strong Muslim community. Sitting and waiting was no option. The Russian Ministry of Defense was given an order to prepare for a military operation in Syria, Russia's first direct combat engagement in an Arab country.

For starters, Russia ramped up dramatically its military aid to Assad's forces. It also sent special operations units to enhance the accuracy of Syrian air strikes. Russia reached out to the potential allies on the ground. In July 2015 Iranian Revolutionary Guard Corps chief General Suleimani reportedly visited Moscow to plan coalition warfare. The agreement was probably sealed during a visit to Tehran by Foreign Minister Sergei Lavrov, who saw Supreme Leader Khamenei. In coordination with Moscow, Tehran dispatched thousands of Shia fighters from Iraq and Afghanistan accompanied by advisers from the Iranian Revolutionary Guards Corps and Basij militias. Iran's Lebanese ally Hezbollah also sent its units to northern Syria.[3] Yet these measures failed to stabilize the situation for Assad's forces.

To the Russian politico-military leadership, developments in Syria were only part of a wider picture. From spring 2015, Moscow became increasingly concerned about the security situation in Central Asia, which was facing leadership transitions in its two key countries, Uzbekistan and Kazakhstan.[4] The situation could worsen, it was believed, as a result of the continuing withdrawal of International Security Assistance Forces from Afghanistan and the rise in Taliban and exiled Central Asian jihadist activities there; of the impact of the IS successes in Syria and Iraq; and of the instability in Tajikistan, which led to a mutiny in its armed forces in early September 2015.

It was the appearance in early 2015 of Islamic State elements in Afghanistan which, for the Russians, carried the biggest threat: unlike the indigenous Taliban movement, which for all its brutality was essentially focused on one country, Afghanistan, IS was composed of a number of groups coming from across Central Asia and China's Xinjiang province. The establishment of an IS branch in "Khorasan," an ancient name for eastern Iran, Afghanistan, and much of Central Asia, sent a signal all the way to the Kremlin.

Through the summer of 2015, against this background, Russian military shipments to Syria achieved unprecedented levels. Moreover, Russia began building infrastructure that suggested it was preparing to step directly into the fight. To close Russia watchers, its military intervention was becoming inevitable.

Observing legalistic formalities has been a hallmark of Vladimir Putin's rule. Russia entered the Syrian conflict at the official request of the Syrian government, by that time boycotted by most Western countries and suspended from the Arab League, but still represented at the United Nations. The two countries were linked by the 1980 treaty on cooperation, which, while not constituting a military alliance, provided for the possibility of military assistance. Bashar al-Assad formally asked for such assistance on September 30, 2015. On the same day, Vladimir Putin accepted the request, and the Federation Council, the upper chamber of the Russian legislature, duly consented to the use of the Russian military forces in Syria. A month before that, Moscow and Damascus had concluded an agreement on the deployment of Russian warplanes in Syria. The planes started to arrive, via Iran and Iraq, in the second half of September.

In late September 2015, Vladimir Putin traveled to New York to attend the seventieth anniversary meeting of the United Nations. From the UN General Assembly platform, he lashed out against U.S. and other Western countries' policies in the Middle East, from the invasion of Iraq through the Arab Spring, asking rhetorically, "Do you realize what you have done?"[5] In the same speech, Putin called on the United States and regional powers in the Middle East to join Russia in a broad antiterrorist coalition.

Growing concern in Washington over the meaning of Russia's military activities in Syria made President Barack Obama, against the advice of his aides, meet with the Kremlin leader when they were both in New York. This was the two presidents' first substantive encounter after the start of the Ukraine crisis and the U.S. announcement of a policy to "isolate Russia." By means of an arms build-up in Syria, Putin effectively made Obama abandon his own course and reach out to him. During the meeting, Putin told Obama he was about to order the

Russian Air Force to begin a military operation in Syria. The first strikes followed less than forty-eight hours later.

War Aims and Strategy

Russia's immediate objective was to forestall the defeat of Bashar al-Assad's forces and the collapse of the Syrian state. A related objective was to prevent battle-hardened jihadists from Russia and the former Soviet republics—numbering up to 7,000 fighters—from returning to their places of origin and destabilizing the situation at home, which logically required killing them in Syria. However, Russia's military engagement in Syria was not only, or even primarily, about Syria or even the Middle East. It had a more global goal.

Coming so soon after the start of the Ukraine crisis, the Syria operation was a second major move by Moscow against the U.S.-dominated world order. Essentially, not only did Russia break again the unspoken post–Cold War taboo on military operations without U.S. consent. It also for the first time went beyond the borders of the former Soviet Union and inserted its military right in the heart of the Middle East. Moreover, Russia acted in support of a government that the United States considered illegitimate, and attacked the forces the U.S. had armed, trained, and funded. It was also the first time ever that Moscow and Washington found themselves directly participating in a war in the same country but on opposite sides. During the Cold War, whether in Korea, Vietnam, or Afghanistan, only one power was actually doing the fighting, while the other was active only indirectly.

Now, the Russian overriding goal was clear—Moscow was seeking a comeback to the global arena as a great power. Any one country capable of pursuing an independent policy, with diplomatic and military means, in the world's most complex and complicated region, such as the Middle East, and achieving a measure of success, fit the description. Russia acted the way it did to make the United States recognize its restored global status. It was not aiming to displace America from the region—Moscow had no interest and no means to fill the void—but rather to get the U.S. acceptance of Russia as a co-equal partner, both politically, through the joint sponsorship of the Syrian reconciliation process, and militarily, by means of joint strikes against IS targets. The latter would have been the first coalition since the end of World War II not run single-handedly by the United States.

Apparently, Russia's war strategy first of all foresaw stabilizing the Assad regime, which meant softening up and throwing back—but not necessarily totally destroying—its non-IS Islamist and secular enemies: these were needed later at the negotiating table with Damascus. Once there, the government and the opposition were expected to eventually agree on a formula of power-sharing in future Syria. These negotiations would be steered and presided over jointly by Russia and the United States. At the initial stage, attacking IS targets—the official objective of Russia's military intervention—would be an important but secondary priority. At the next stage, once the political process got under way, Russia and the United States would join forces against the IS, the results of the strikes exploited on the ground by the Syrian government and opposition forces, and the Kurds.

By deciding to go into Syria, the Russian leadership got rid of the "Afghan syndrome" that barred intervention in a foreign Muslim-populated country. The Kremlin made sure, however, that the Syria expedition should not be subject to an escalation, a mission creep, or a quagmire, and clearly defined its parameters and limitations. By aligning Russia with the Syrian Alawite regime, Iran, and Iraq, as well as Hezbollah, Putin did not shy away from a potential conflict with the Sunni world outside and inside Russia, where Sunni Muslims constituted a vast majority. He reached out to all the major Sunni states in the region and to the Muslim community in Russia itself,[6] where he visited the opening of the country's biggest mosque, in Moscow, on the eve of the Syrian operation.

Air War

By the standards of Russian warfighting, the Syria operation has been very unusual. It is being conducted primarily by the Air Space Forces, as the Russian Air Force had come to be known since August 2015. The air arm of the military is being assisted by the Navy, which fired cruise missiles into Syria from the Caspian and the Mediterranean Seas, and brought its own air elements and air defenses to Syria's shores. The Ground Forces, by contrast, have been expressly excluded from the battlefield, reflecting Putin's reluctance to be drawn into ground combat in a Muslim country: clearly, the lesson of Afghanistan had been learned. To be sure, there were Russian military personnel on the ground, but they did not come anywhere close to the levels of involvement in the fighting seen in Afghanistan or Chechnya.

War

The Russian air contingent in Syria was relatively small. It initially included twelve Su-24M theater bombers; an equal number of Su-25SM ground attack aircraft; four Su-34 theater bombers; four Su-30SM fighters; one Il-20M1 radio reconnaissance plane; twelve Mi-24P combat helicopters; and five Mi-8AMTSh transport helicopters—a total of thirty-two combat planes, plus eighteen other aircraft. By February 2016 their number had peaked at forty-four, but in March was reduced to twenty-four, when Putin announced a partial pullout of Russian forces from Syria. Later, the numbers continued to fluctuate, but the force itself remained numerically modest.

Drawn from different units across Russia, this group was formally organized as a special purpose air brigade, based at the Hmeimim air base just southwest of Latakia City.[7] Apart from the planes based in Syria itself, Russia employed its Long-Range Aviation force operating from its bases on the Volga River, the North Caucasus, and even as far as the Kola Peninsula. In this way, Cold War–era Tu-160 and Tu-95MS strategic bombers were used in combat operations for the first time. Russia's A-50 AWACS planes, based in the North Caucasus, were also in the air to monitor the situation. This allowed the Russian Air Space Force to test its readiness and capabilities across its various branches and units.

The Russian Navy first got into the Syrian fray from the Caspian, where in October 2015 it fired cruise missiles from a distance of 1,500 kilometers, and then from the Mediterranean, where a Russian submarine fired cruise missiles. In the fall of 2016, a Russian aircraft carrier, the *Admiral Kuznetsov*, sailed from Severomorsk to Syria to be used as a platform for combat sorties, and stayed in the area until the capture of Aleppo in December 2016 by Syrian government forces. Even before that, the missile cruiser *Moskva* had brought the S-300F air defense system to Syria's shores. Like the Air Space Force, the Russian navy employed ships drawn from all of its fleets: the Black Sea, Northern, Baltic, and Pacific.

The Russian forces on the ground, around 3,000–4,000 strong, are there primarily to protect the air base. They are drawn from the Special Operations Forces, the Marines, mountain assault units, and the Ground Forces proper. They are armed with T-90 main battle tanks, 152 mm towed howitzers, and a number of air defense systems, including the S-400, the most advanced in the Russian arsenal. After the fall of Aleppo, Russia sent a battalion of its recently formed military police into the city.

Separate from these forces are some artillery crews and a number of advisers embedded with the Syrian government forces.

Operating at a distance from Russia's borders, this expeditionary contingent has been supplied by air initially across Iran and Iraq, more recently also across Turkey. However, the main supply line runs by sea from Novorossiysk and Sevastopol on the Black Sea to Syria's Tartus: the so-called Syria Express. At its maximum, Russia, using both routes, was sending 2,500 tons of military cargo per day.[8]

The Russian air strikes were initially mostly aimed (80 percent or so) at the Islamist and secular rebel formations around Damascus, Latakia, and Hama. These rebels were supported by Turkey, the Gulf States and the West. The Russian strikes allowed the Syrian government forces to launch counter-attacks in the Hama area, but their gains were only tactical, and were soon reversed. The Syrians and their Russian allies were more successful in the Latakia province, which hosted the Hmeimim air-base, the center of their military operations. The main focus of the Syrian government's war effort, assisted by the Iranians, was Aleppo. In November 2015, the Russian air support allowed Assad's forces to relieve the siege of the Kwaires airfield. Eastern Aleppo, however, remained a stronghold of the Islamist opposition until its fall more than a year later.

Although the Russian military operation in Syria was billed from the start as "anti-terrorist," it was mostly directed against Assad's various armed opponents rather than the Islamic State group. This was fully consistent with the immediate objective of the Russian military operation in Syria: to stabilize the Assad regime, which was besieged by the forces of the opposition, not those of IS. Faced with criticism from the United States and other Western governments and the Western and Arab media, Moscow maintained that many among Assad's non-IS opponents were nothing but terrorists. As Sergei Lavrov commented right after the Putin-Obama meeting in New York, if "someone walks like a terrorist, and acts like a terrorist, he is a terrorist."[9] IS targets were also engaged, particularly with the purpose of destroying its oil trade and thus stifling IS financially.

When he announced the operation, President Putin said it would be limited not only in scope, but also in time. This plan eventually worked, but not immediately. The two ceasefires between Damascus and the opposition, negotiated with Russian and U.S. backing in February and then in September 2016, were broken. It was only after Russia had supported the Syrian government's seizure of

Aleppo toward the end of 2016, and had engineered a new truce with the help of Turkey, that military success could be translated into a serious political negotiation.

In 2015–2016, the Russian forces, operating mostly in the air, achieved greater results with fewer casualties than in almost any other military campaign that Moscow had waged. In the first nine months of the operation, the Russian aircraft made over 11,000 sorties while losing only one combat plane—as a result of the Turkish attack. There were also only a few losses due to equipment malfunctioning. Logistical support was rated as "outstanding." The Air Space Forces have demonstrated a high degree of combat readiness and a capacity to wage high-intensity operations.[10]

The operation in Syria allowed the Russian armed forces to combat-test new weapons systems, such as the Su-30, Su-34, and Su-35, and the *Kalibr* sea-launched long-range cruise missile. When Russian officials compared the cost of the Syria operation to that of a continuous military exercise, they were right on target: the operation has become an ongoing exercise, where weapons systems are tested and servicemen get their combat training. Russia's air war, however, would not have made much sense without coordination with the friendly forces fighting on the ground. Success in Syria depended on the capacity and cohesion of the Moscow-led coalition.

Coalition Warfare

The war in Syria has become, to Russia, a coalition effort to a far larger extent than the Soviet war in Afghanistan was. Besides the Syrian Arab Army and other local pro-Assad forces, Russia needed to coordinate its efforts with the Iranians and their allies. Moscow also had to coordinate with Baghdad, whose airspace was vital for Russian strategic bombers and cruise missile strikes. In Baghdad, a Russo-Iranian-Syrian-Iraqi coordination center was set up for the purpose.

Moscow's alliance with Damascus was never perfect. Russia supported Assad as the central pillar of the Syrian state, a rare Arab leader who refused to capitulate before an uprising, and someone who was sufficiently dependent on Moscow and thus an instrument of Russia's regional and global policies. That said, the Russians were not fans of Assad's inflexible and repressive domestic politics, and were exasperated by the Syrian president's refusal to follow their advice to take a more conciliatory stance toward his opponents. In 2012–14, Moscow sought to engage closely with the opposition in an effort to reach a political settlement in Syria, an effort often stymied by Damascus, fearful that a success of that effort would bring an end to Assad's rule.

Yet in 2015 Russia and Syria became military allies in the full sense of the word. Syria gave the Russians the right to use an air base for an indefinite period, and extended the lease on the naval facility for forty-nine years, while Russian air strikes killed the enemies of the regime in Damascus. The Syrian air defense units were integrated with the more capable Russian systems under a single command.

Yet even after Russia's entry into war in 2015, Moscow and Damascus did not always see eye to eye. Sergei Lavrov quipped that Syria was not the kind of ally to Russia that Turkey was to the United States.[11] The Kremlin was unhappy with Assad's strategy of being either too ambivalent or too unrealistic. The Russian leadership did not share Assad's goal of clearing all of Syria of his enemies. A few weeks after the start of the air campaign, Putin had to summon Assad to Moscow, where he was delivered on board a Russian military plane for a serious conversation in the Kremlin. At another juncture, Putin sent Defense Minister Sergei Shoigu to Syria to tell Damascus to get its act together. However,

Russia rejected from the start the opposition demand that Assad step down as a precondition to negotiations.

During the war, Russian public criticism of the Syrian government's battlefield efforts was muted, but the fall in December 2016 of Palmyra, liberated from IS with Russia's air and artillery support to much fanfare the previous March, led to some airing on Russian state TV of military experts' anxiety about the Syrian ally, its complacency, inefficiency, and cooperation with the enemy.[12] At the Astana talks between Damascus and the opposition, held from January 2017, Moscow sought to take the position of a neutral facilitator of the Syrian peace process. This hardly made Assad happy. He took a hard line at the peace talks and continued to put pressure on the opposition on the battlefield. The opposition, for its part, continued to insist on Assad's departure, which led to breaches of the ceasefire and made Russia resume its air support for Damascus's army. Assad was also able to play Russia off Iran, his only other ally.

Predictably, Iran, with its 7,000 men on the ground in Syria, has turned out to be a difficult ally. Historically, as described in Chapter 1, Russo-Persian relations were often tense and virtually never close. In Syria, however, there was a substantial overlap of interests between Moscow and Tehran: neither wanted Assad to fall at the hands of the local opposition, the United States, or IS. This created a fairly solid basis for cooperation. Russia and Iran have managed to coordinate their military efforts in Syria reasonably well. The Iranians allowed the use of its airspace by the Russian planes and cruise missiles en route to Syria. Even several missiles crashing in Iran (without creating damage) did not strain the relationship.

Beyond that, however, Russian and Iranian objectives in Syria differed. Whereas Tehran sought to keep the Alawites in power in Damascus as part of its drive for regional predominance, extending Tehran's reach to the Mediterranean coast (including a naval base) and the borders of Israel (including near the Golan Heights), Moscow was aiming for a compromise deal involving power-sharing among different groups in Syria, as long as these groups recognized Russia's role in the Middle East and its presence in the country. Moscow certainly did not share Tehran's agenda either in the Gulf or in Yemen. In the latter case, Russia, while criticizing the Saudi-led intervention, did not condemn the Saudis and their allies too harshly, pleading instead for a political settlement to end the war in Yemen.

Iran is also wary of surrendering even a small portion of its sovereignty to a foreign power. When in mid-August 2016 it allowed Russia to use its Shahid Noje air base north of Hamadan for strikes in Syria, this created an uproar in Tehran, fed in part by the Russian media characterizing the agreement as Russia getting another air base in the Middle East, after Syria's Hmeimim. Within a few days, Russian air sorties from Hamadan were discontinued. Iranians were generally unhappy that Russia did not give them enough credit publicly for their land operations, while hyping their own air strikes.

Iraq's role in the joint war effort is mainly as a land and air corridor for Iranian forces going to or from the Syrian battlefield. Russian planes and cruise missiles also flew over Iraq to their targets in Syria. Baghdad hosts the intelligence exchange and coordination center for Russian, Syrian, Iranian, and Iraqi militaries. It was in Baghdad that the Russian general on that center visited the U.S. defense attaché on September 30, 2015, to advise him of the imminent Russian air campaign in Syria and the need to keep off the Russian planes' flight paths. However, Russians have to acknowledge the limitations of their cooperation with Iraq, due to Baghdad's security dependence on and close ties with Washington.

After the truce with the opposition, the Russians focused virtually exclusively on fighting IS. This brought together a different coalition of powers. From January 2017, Russian planes began to support Turkey's offensive, particularly in the El-Bab area of northern Syria, which required closer interaction with the Turkish military. In March 2017, Russian and U.S. forces found themselves within a few miles of each other in the area of Manbij, another key city held by IS. Even in the absence of a formal coalition, the U.S. and Russian top military officers met face-to-face in February and March 2017 to discuss coordination.

Casualties

By early March 2017, Russian losses in Syria had numbered twenty-eight people.[13] Almost two months into the Russian operation, on November 24, 2015, a Russian Su-24 bomber was shot down near the Syrian-Turkish border by Turkey's F-16 fighter. The pilot, who catapulted, was killed in the air by pro-Turkish militants in the area. A Russian marine on a rescue mission was also killed. The two men became the first Russian combat casualties in the Syrian war. Not all casualties, however, were sustained on the battlefield, or included military personnel.

Exactly a month after the start of the Russian air campaign, a Russian passenger plane exploded over the Sinai Peninsula, killing all 224 people on board. This was certified as an act of terrorism perpetrated by an extremist cell in Sinai allied to IS. In view of some, this was a response to the Russian military operation in Syria; others, however, believed it was unrelated. In December 2016, a former Turkish police officer killed Russia's ambassador in Ankara, Andrei Karlov, in revenge for the bombing of Aleppo. This was the first assassination of a Moscow ambassador abroad in almost ninety years.

From the start of the air campaign, there have been obvious fears of terrorist attacks inside Russia. Threats of mega-terrorism with mass civilian casualties remain real. A number of attacks—as many as fifty in 2016—have been uncovered and prevented by the Russian security services. A number of shootings and bombings did take place in the restless North Caucasus. Some perpetrators expressed allegiance to IS. It is difficult to say, however, whether these attacks were a result of the Syria operation. Russia was not spared acts of terrorism even when it was not engaged in conflicts in the Middle East. In April 2017, terrorists struck in the St. Petersburg metro, killing fifteen people and injuring scores of others in the first-ever such attack in Russia's second capital, timed to coincide with President Putin's visit to the city. This was the first major act of terrorism in Russia since 2013. Naturalized Central Asian immigrants linked to IS were suspected.

Any war is a cruel thing. Beyond doubt, Russian air strikes also killed a number of Syrian civilians, and destroyed their homes and livelihoods. In particular, the 2016 bombardment of Aleppo was described by the Syrian opposition and the U.S., British, and French governments as a war crime, for which the Syrian government and its Russian ally were held responsible. Moscow angrily rejected the accusation, specifically any premeditated hits of hospitals and schools, saying that the charges were unfounded, and coming from terrorists or their allies. For their part, the Russians pointed to the massive loss of life among the residents of Mosul as a result of the U.S.-led coalition bombardment in early 2017. This bitter exchange was certainly a case of information warfare.

It is certainly true that there is no military need to destroy schools and hospitals, but it is equally true that any civilian casualties in a modern war are immediately turned into a propaganda weapon by the opposing side. This is true of U.S., Israeli, or

Saudi attacks in various parts of the Middle East, from Iraq to Syria to Yemen, and it is also true about Russia's in Syria. It is also a well-known fact that the weaker party in a war, such as Hamas in Gaza, IS in Iraq, or the Syrian opposition, seeks to hit back at its enemy through global public opinion, and usually finds outlets interested in broadcasting the footage. Using civilians as a human shield is a time-tested tactic.

At the cost of the equivalent of $4 million a day, the military intervention in Syria has been reasonably affordable to the Russian budget. The payoff from the war included powerful advertisements both for Russia's weapons systems and for Moscow's political backing. Neither was lost on Middle Eastern leaders. Russia, which had not been on the agenda of many Arab leaders for a long time, reentered their calculations. The boost in global prestige was more difficult to calculate, but it was just as real.

War and Peace

From the start, the Russian military operation was supposed to be limited in scope, time, weapons, and tactics used. By late February 2016 it seemed that

Moscow's strategy would bear fruit. Immediately following the launch of the Russian air campaign, U.S. secretary of state John Kerry began working closely with Russian foreign minister Sergei Lavrov to find a political solution to the Syria conflict. Over the next twelve months, the two met two dozen times and also spent long hours communicating by phone.

Russia and the United States, as co-chairs of the International Syria Support Group, negotiated a cessation of hostilities between the Syrian government forces and the opposition, except for IS and Nusra. The ceasefire agreement, supported by the UN Security Council, was to be monitored by a Russian reconciliation center at Hmeimim and a U.S. Military Operations Command in Amman, Jordan. Things, however, turned out to be more difficult than originally expected.

Russia's goal was not helping Assad to achieve a complete military victory that was considered impossible. It hoped to use the ceasefire to separate hardline irreconcilable opponents of the regime from those who could be swayed toward reconciliation. The latter would receive humanitarian aid; the former would be attacked and bombed. The ceasefire also allowed the relaunch in Geneva of indirect political talks between Damascus and the various opposition groups mediated by the UN secretary general's special envoy, Staffan de Mistura.

The talks, however, stalled. The so-called Riyadh group of the opposition withdrew from the dialogue in protest against the government's actions in the Aleppo area, which also blocked humanitarian aid. Damascus rejected any notion of federalization of Syria, refused to agree to the Kurds' participation, and staged parliamentary elections in the territory it controlled. Exasperated with Assad, Sergei Lavrov publicly stated that "Assad is not our ally.... We support him in the fight against terrorism and in the preservation of the Syrian state. But he is not an ally in the same sense as Turkey is a U.S. ally."[14] Ankara, too, was blocking the Kurdish participation in the Geneva talks.

By August 2016, the ceasefire, which had never been fully observed, fell through. The following month, Russia and the United States agreed in Geneva on a new ceasefire. However, it was broken again within a couple of weeks. First, the U.S. Air Force, by mistake, as it later said, attacked Syrian government forces in Deir-ez-Zor, killing dozens of personnel; then, a Red Crescent humanitarian convoy traveling to opposition-held eastern Aleppo was attacked and burned, with a number of aid workers killed. This attack was blamed on the

Syrian or Russian air forces, though both denied responsibility. The Obama administration stopped cooperation with Russia on Syria.

From Moscow's perspective, however, that cooperation failed to yield results due to the U.S. inability to separate the Nusra fighters from the rest of the opposition and, more seriously, because of the disagreements within Washington regarding the wisdom of cooperating with Russia. While John Kerry advocated such cooperation, the Pentagon and the intelligence community were highly negative on it, and the president himself was ambivalent. In the end, Russia turned to Turkey as a partner, and in December 2016, following the capture of eastern Aleppo, negotiated a ceasefire with Ankara's help. This allowed peace talks to restart in January 2017, under the auspices of Moscow, Ankara, and Tehran—with the United States as an observer—given the delay in the formation of a new U.S. administration. Although cheered by some Russians, the apparent U.S. demotion has never been the objective of the Kremlin's policy. Rather, Moscow *needed* Washington at its side to witness and confirm Russia's reappearance on the global stage as a great power.

Meanwhile, Russia's biggest issues are with its nominal partners, Iran and Turkey, as well as

Damascus and the opposition, whom Moscow has by now upgraded from "terrorists" to "field commanders." Transforming oneself from an ally of the Syrian regime into an impartial facilitator of the peace process and the guarantor of an eventual agreement will not be easy for Russia. Its relations with Tehran and Damascus will be particularly sensitive—in the situation when Assad will try to play Iran off Russia. Russia will also need to come to terms with the Saudis and the Qataris, who are not formally involved in the peace process. In April 2017 Damascus was accused of a chemical attack in Idlib province, for the first time since the Syrian chemical weapons arsenal had been declared eliminated. Russia, which stood by Assad in rejecting the claim, was clearly embarrassed. The United States responded with a strike against a Syrian airfield—its first direct military engagement in the war. Essentially, Moscow faced the choice between being used by Assad in pursuit of the mirage of a full victory, or trying to rein him in, risking the collapse of the coalition with Damascus and a loss of influence there to Tehran.

War

Preliminary Results

As a provisional result of its Syria campaign, Russia has come back as a major geopolitical player and a capable military actor in the Middle East. It prevented the outcomes it found dangerous: the toppling of the regime in Damascus by Islamists or as a result of a U.S. intervention. Its air strikes killed a number of IS fighters of Russian/former Soviet origin. It helped Damascus to fight the opposition to the negotiating table. It won air and naval basing rights in Syria. Thus, Russia did away with the U.S. monopoly on political and military action in the Middle East. The Russian military proved to be an effective tool of Moscow's foreign policy. Russia also managed to achieve these spectacular results with very limited military and financial resources.

Moscow also emerged from its military engagement in Syria as the player with the most connections in the region. During the war, President Putin stayed in close touch with virtually all regional leaders, including those of Turkey, Iran, Israel, Egypt, Saudi Arabia, the United Arab Emirates, Qatar, Kuwait, Bahrain, Jordan, and Lebanon. Russia managed to avoid the risk of falling into the cracks of Middle Eastern divides: Shia versus Sunni; Saudi versus Iran; Iran versus Israel; Turkey versus the Kurds, and so on. It is this ability to promote one's interest in a conflict-infested environment that is particularly useful for a country aiming to be a global player. It is negotiating those divides that would test Russia's ability not only to promote its own interests, but also to deliver public goods—a mark of a true great power in the twenty-first century.

3

Diplomacy

Military action is only effective as long as it furthers a general political strategy. In Syria, there was a very close connection between Russia's military operation and its diplomatic activity. While Moscow does not have a grand strategy *for* the Middle East, it has a clear view of its interests in specific situations within the region. In pursuit of those interests, it has managed to deal with countries and groups that have often been inimical to one another, and even sometimes to bring them together, as a public good. This chapter deals with Russia's way of negotiating intra-regional divides in different parts of the Middle East—in the form of mini-case studies.

Diplomacy

Russia and the Israeli-Palestinian Conflict

During the Cold War, the Soviet Union was fully on the side of Arab states and the Palestinians; Israel was an adversary. "Zionists" were treated as allies of American imperialism. After the end of the Cold War, this changed dramatically. In 1991, the Soviet Union reestablished diplomatic relations with Israel. Even though the Russian Federation was too weak to play a significant role in the Israeli-Palestinian dialogue, Russia has been part of the Middle East Quartet, alongside the United States, the European Union, and the United Nations. For a long time, Russia was happy to let the United States drive the process of reconciliation. The Oslo accords and the Middle East peace process were largely off its agenda, for a period of time.

During that period, a new balance was formed in Russia's approach to the issue. Even as Russia's relations with Israel were mended, those with the Palestinians stagnated. Moscow did not switch sides. Instead, it became even-handed. While Russia generally voted with the Arabs at the UN, it built at the same time an increasingly deeper understanding with Israel. The Chechen war was a crucial factor there. Essentially, Russians felt that they and the Israelis were confronted with the same kind of enemy: radicalized Muslims going to extremes, including terrorism. In the North Caucasus during the 1990s, there were numerous Arab radicals, financed by Arab sources, fighting against the Russian Federation.

Then, there was demographics. Those Jews who emigrated to Israel from the Soviet Union, as it broke apart, became a human bridge to Russia and a link between Israeli and Russian establishments. These people were very different from average post-Soviet emigrés in the West who mostly despised their country of origin. Numbering about 1 million in a country of 6 million, these people continue to speak Russian. A strong and politically influential group, they favor maintaining ties to Russia. Within Russia itself, these people are seen as near-compatriots. They are ubiquitous on Russian TV and in the other mass media, and their views, including on the situation in the Middle East, are widely disseminated within Russia.

Moscow leaders, rather anti-Israeli from the 1950s until the 1980s, have markedly warmed up to the Jewish state. Mikhail Gorbachev broke with the history of official antisemitism; Boris Yeltsin rebuilt relations with Israel; and Vladimir Putin is the most pro-Israel, pro-Jewish leader Russia has ever known. As far as Putin is concerned, some of this is personal, originating with his teachers and friends of his youth, but much comes from his rational understanding of the scope and scale of Jewish influence in the United States and Western Europe. Putin regularly meets with leaders of the Russian Jewish community. His protégé, Mikhail Fradkov, served as Russia's first-ever Jewish prime minister and head of the country's Foreign Intelligence Service (SVR). Judaism has been officially made one of four "indigenous religions" in Russia, alongside Orthodox Christianity, Islam, and Buddhism. Putin reveres the memory of the Holocaust. He visited Auschwitz in Poland and helped establish a Holocaust museum in Moscow. Shared memories of World War II play an important part in the new Russian-Israeli relations. A number of Soviet war veterans of Jewish origin who went to live in Israel are very proud of their service.

For Russian military and security services, once the home of everyday antisemitism, Israel has become a model of efficiency, determination, national solidarity, social cohesion, and a willingness to persevere and move forward against all odds—if necessary, alone against the rest of the world. In more practical ways, they also see Israel as a source of high technology. Russian and Israeli politicians and generals share a no-nonsense, hard-nosed *Realpolitik*-based view of the world. Unlike most Americans and Europeans, they never thought much, for example, of the democratic prospects of the Arab Spring.

For ordinary Russians, Israel is the one country in the Middle East where they may feel virtually at home. Russian is widely spoken and understood; it is the language of a number of TV channels, newspapers, and theaters. Those who can afford it come to Israel for world-class medical treatment, usually provided by Russian-speaking doctors and personnel. For Russian Christian Orthodox believers, Israel is the Holy Land, to which they pay pilgrimage. For tourists, Israel is the seat of ancient civilization, epitomized by Jerusalem. Russian beachgoers prefer Eilat. Since 2008, no visas are required between the two countries.

Post-Soviet Russia's ties to the Palestinians are not nearly as rich and strong as those with Israel, but they are perfectly functional. No longer a sponsor of the PLO, which is now mainly supported by the European Union, Moscow has continued to keep contacts with Yasser Arafat and, after his death, with Mahmoud Abbas, Arafat's successor as president of the Palestinian Authority. Having formally recognized the "State of Palestine" as far back as 1982, Moscow keeps a diplomatic presence in Ramallah. When Russian leaders visit Israel, they usually make a point of going to the Palestinian territories to speak with top PLO officials. As in Israel, Christian sites on the West Bank, starting with Bethlehem, are places of pilgrimage by Russian believers, and some of them are looked after by the Russian Orthodox Church.

After the Fatah-Hamas split in 2006, and the elections in Gaza that brought Hamas to power, Moscow took a pragmatic stance toward the intra-Palestinian dispute. The Foreign Ministry invited Hamas leaders to Russia and has maintained dialogue with them ever since. Initially, the move was strongly criticized by Israel and the bulk of the Western media. The Russians were accused of legitimizing terrorists. Moscow, however, stayed the course. Besides maintaining contacts with a group popularly elected to govern a nearly two-million-strong territory, the Russians have tried to facilitate a degree of reconciliation between the two rival Palestinian factions. This has relevance and potential value to Israel: no Israeli-Palestinian accord is feasible without an intra-Palestinian agreement beforehand.

Russia prides itself in having taken a more balanced attitude toward the parties to the Israeli-Palestinian dispute than any other outside player. Moreover, no longer relaxed to leave the Middle

East peace process in the solitary care of the United States, Russia is now seeking to play a more prominent role in the Quartet. Its general view is that the Israeli-Palestinian issues need to be resolved by the two parties themselves, in a direct dialogue. While Moscow considers Jewish settlements in the West Bank illegal, it finds Palestinian attempts to reverse the situation by appealing to the international community unproductive. Advertising itself as a responsible "Quartet" member, Russia has been signaling its readiness to host an Israeli-Palestinian dialogue in Moscow. This idea, first put forward by Vladimir Putin during his trip to the Middle East in 2005, has been kept alive ever since. If Moscow ever succeeds in its ambition of hosting peace talks between Israel and the Palestinians, Russia's diplomatic standing in the region will soar. Alas, the two parties are very far away from resolving their seventy-year-long dispute.

Israel-Syria

From the 1960s through the 1980s, Syria was Moscow's closest ally in the Middle East, and Israel, its most likely regional opponent—apart from NATO member Turkey. The Soviet Union built up the Syrian army to deter the Israelis, even though it did not accede to Damascus's demands to give it more sophisticated weapons. Yet after the end of the Cold War, Russia stopped considering Syria as an ally and Israel as an adversary. With no control over Assad's policies, it did not feel obligated to shield Syria from Israeli strikes aimed at its missile or WMD facilities (as in 2007), or at weapons shipments to the Lebanese Shiite politico-military organization, Hezbollah.

From the start in 2015 of the military operation, when it came to the rescue of Damascus and the Syrian state, Russia has stayed in close touch with Israel. It made sure that Israel did not feel threatened by the arrival of Russian planes and air defense systems in Latakia province. It took measures to de-conflict Russian and Israeli air movements and operations. Constant contact between the two militaries and security services has so far excluded incidents.

Russia understands Israel's security concerns. In 2005, Putin acceded to a personal request from Prime Minister Ehud Olmert to cancel the sale of Iskander missiles to Damascus, and in 2013 to a similar request from Prime Minister Binyamin Netanyahu regarding the S-300 air defense systems. Moscow did not provide Hezbollah with weapons and insisted that the weapons it had transferred to Damascus did not get passed on to Hezbollah. Russia did not protest strongly against Israeli air strikes in Syria, hitting Hezbollah targets. From Moscow's perspective, once the war in Syria is over, Hezbollah fighters should return to Lebanon. Should it eventually come to a peace settlement between Israel and Syria, Russia is best placed to act as a facilitator of that difficult dialogue.

Thus, while Syria has become Russia's most important stronghold in the Middle East, Israel has emerged as an important and in many respects unique partner for Russia in the region. Russian and Israeli leaders meet frequently, speak candidly with each other, and use largely the same terms of reference. Neither Russia nor Israel, of course, sees the other country as an ally. There are clearly no obligations that tie Russia to Israel, as in the case of the U.S.-Israeli relations. The relationship is squarely based on the national interests of the parties. This provides a degree of stability to the relationship, allowing it to withstand major differences, such as on Iran.

Diplomacy

Iran and Israel

As one of the historical guardians of global strategic stability and the nuclear non-proliferation regime, Moscow has consistently opposed Iran becoming a nuclear weapons state. Russia participated in the negotiations on the Iranian nuclear program as part of the P5+1 concert. It did not change its position or break out of the format even as the Russian-American relations deteriorated to the level of confrontation in 2014. Such principled Russian attitude allowed the Joint Comprehensive Plan of Action (JCPOA) to be signed in July 2015.

While staunchly advocating nuclear non-proliferation, however, Russia has always been skeptical about Israel's alarmism toward Iran's nuclear programs. Moscow saw Iranians as essentially rational, even if it did not support Tehran's nuclear or regional ambitions. In the Russian analysis, if a country of Iran's size, potential, self-image, and history wanted to go nuclear, it would reach that goal, and no one in the world would be in a position to prevent it—except by means of a major war, long-term occupation of Iran, total replacement of its elite, and similar unrealistic conditions—like those imposed on Germany after 1945. Military strikes against Iran, the Russian thinking went, would only postpone the nuclear program, but they also would make sure that it continued through the development and production stages and all the way to deployment of Iran's nuclear weapons. The only way to ensure that Iran renounced the nuclear weapons option was to reach a deal with Tehran giving it security reassurance and free access to global trade and finances. The Russians are basically happy with what has been achieved by means of the JCPOA.

Former Iranian president Mahmoud Ahmadinejad's fiery rhetoric did not endear him to Putin and Medvedev, but it did not scare them either. Russians saw Iran as a complex society with a very elaborate political system with its own countervailing trends. Moscow's own experience with Iranian leaders suggested that they may be difficult to deal with, but that there was a way of managing with them, based on the national—or corporate, personal, etc.—interest. Their favorite counterpart in Tehran was the late President Hashemi Rafsandjani, the wheeler-dealer politician who managed to drive a bargain across the entire political spectrum of the country: an epitome of "eternal Persia" to the Russians.

Of course, medieval Persia to the Russians is not the same thing as ancient Persia to the Israelis. To be fair, the Russians took into account those

Iranian and Israeli security concerns they deemed legitimate. In 2010, at the height of Ahmadinejad's anti-Israel rhetoric, they suspended the delivery of the already paid-for S-300 air defense system to Iran. From 2015 on, while fighting alongside the Iranians in Syria, the Russians have been careful to closely coordinate their movements in the air with the Israelis, for the purposes of reassurance and de-confliction. For its part, Israel abstained during the UN General Assembly vote in March 2014 condemning Russia's annexation of Crimea and did not join the U.S.-led economic sanctions against Moscow.

With the talks about a future political settlement in Syria reactivated after the ceasefire achieved in December 2016, Netanyahu pleaded with Putin not to allow an Iranian military presence in Syria, particularly in the form of a naval base on the Mediterranean and Hezbollah or Iraqi Shiite formations on the Golan Heights. While Russia will not allow Israel—or the United States, for that matter—to have a veto on its relations with Iran, it will probably work for a Syria free from foreign military presence, except its own, of course.

Diplomacy

Iran and Turkey

Iran and Turkey are Russia's two semi-direct neighbors, across the Black Sea and the Caspian. The small states that now separate Russia from those two regional powers were largely conquered by the Russian Empire from the Ottoman sultans and the Persian shahs. While realizing of course that Iran and Turkey are historical rivals, Russians need them both as partners in an effort to prevent a large-scale destabilization of the region.

In the Syria conflict, Iran and Turkey have clearly different interests. At the beginning of Russia's air campaign, Tehran was an ally of Moscow, and Ankara, particularly after the Turks shot down a Russian bomber in November 2015, was almost an enemy. Yet as Turkey redefined its policies in mid-2016 and then began to work closely with Russia, Moscow, Ankara, and Tehran found themselves on the same side. In December 2016, Russia staged a trilateral ministerial meeting in Moscow, designed to form a diplomatic coalition to end the fighting in Syria. This led to the agreement between Damascus and the Syrian opposition, brokered by Moscow and Ankara, and notionally supported by Tehran, to hold talks in Astana, Kazakhstan.

However, this diplomatic "trio" is in fact a "two plus one" construct. In December 2016, Turkey played the key part in ending of the siege of Eastern Aleppo and evacuating the remaining rebels and civilians from there, after which the city came under the Syrian government control. In January 2017, Russia and Turkey formed a military coalition to jointly fight IS forces near El Bab. With regard to the future of Syria, Ankara essentially acquiesced in supporting the Russian approach toward the country's constitutional transformation toward a decentralized polity within the present borders.

Iran's position, by contrast, is far less flexible. Tehran wants to keep the "land bridge" that links it across Iraq to Syria and Lebanon, and it firmly stands by the Assad clan and the ruling Alawites as its only allies in Sunni-majority Syria. In order not to be taken for granted, Tehran objected to Moscow's invitation of the United States to participate in the Astana talks. To the Russians, this is hardly surprising. They also saw this before—in the Turkish president Recep Tayyip Erdogan's hardline approach toward removing Assad from power. They also found means to help the Turks scale down their demands. They may find an equally effective approach to the Iranians to make them accept less than what they demand.

Diplomacy

Turkey and the Kurds

Russia's entry into the Syria war fatally undercut Turkey's policy in that country. Turkey's allies in Syria were being destroyed by Russian strikes, and the arrival of the Russian air defense system deterred Ankara from action in their defense. There could be no question any more of Turkey invading Syria, forming security areas there, and declaring a no-fly zone, not to speak of the moves to topple Bashar al-Assad in Damascus. In this environment, the downing of the Russian bomber by Turkish fighters in November 2015 was not an isolated incident, and it had more to do with Russia's policies in Syria than any violation of the Turkish airspace.

In response to the downing of its plane and the death of its pilot at the hands of the pro-Turkish militants, Moscow refrained from hitting back militarily, but placed Ankara and President Erdogan under heavy pressure: economic, political, and informational. In February 2016 it allowed the Syrian Kurdish party PYD, which Ankara regarded as an ally of the Kurdistan Workers' Party (PKK, dubbed a terrorist group in Turkey), to establish an office in the Russian capital. PYD's military wing, YPG, received some Russian aid. Kremlin-connected commentators began to talk positively about the struggle that Kurdish activists and militants were waging in Turkey itself. Even though Moscow stopped short of officially endorsing the PKK, the message was not to be mistaken.

It was not the first time that Russia used the Kurdish issue to pressure the Turks. In the mid-1990s, as it sought to counter Turkish interference in the North Caucasus and the restrictions Ankara imposed on Russian commercial traffic in the Straits, Moscow allowed PKK to open an office in Russia. Abdullah Ocalan, the Kurdish leader, was permitted to stay in Russia for a period of time. The Kurdish card worked again.

Eventually, by July 2016 Turkey relented and Erdogan apologized to Putin for the death of the pilot and the loss of the plane. Putin, for his part, supported Erdogan during the failed coup that same month. In August 2016, Erdogan flew to St. Petersburg for a reconciliation meeting with Putin. The Russian leader accepted the apology and moved ahead to involve Ankara in Moscow's strategy for Syria. Essentially, in exchange for Turkey's willingness to follow Russia's lead on Syria, Putin agreed to take Turkey's security interests into account. Soon after the Putin-Erdogan encounter, Turkey mounted the "Shield of the Euphrates" operation in northern Syria, designed primarily to prevent the creation of a Kurdish enclave all along its border. Although obviously undertaken without Damascus's approval, the operation did not provoke Moscow's condemnation as it had probably been approved by Putin in his meeting with Erdogan. Toward the end of 2016 and in early 2017, when Turkey engaged in fighting IS formations, Russia joined the fight, bombing IS positions in the area. When in January 2017 a bombing raid in support of the Turkish military and its allies resulted in the death of three Turkish soldiers and wounding of several others, Putin promptly apologized. The incident produced no crisis in Russian-Turkish relations.

As for the broader issue of Kurdish independence, Russia has been both pragmatic and cautious. It has maintained historically close contacts with Kurdish leaders in both Syria and Iraq. Former foreign minister Evgeny Primakov used to cultivate the Kurdish nationalist leader Mustafa Barzani as far back as the 1970s. In 2007, Russia established a consulate in Erbil, the capital of the Kurdistan Regional Government (KRG) in northern Iraq. Gazprom Neft won oil drilling rights in KRG territory. Yet keeping the current borders in the Middle East intact remains Russia's basic position. There, Russia is painstakingly maintaining balance. Even as it reaches out to the KRG or the Syrian Kurds, who in 2016 proclaimed their own republic, Moscow seeks to reassure the governments in Baghdad and Damascus that it is not questioning their countries' territorial integrity. In its draft Constitution of Syria handed over to the Syrian opposition in Astana, Russia backed autonomy for Syria's Kurds.

Shia-Sunni, Iran, and the Gulf States

When Russia intervened in Syria in 2015, there were hopes and fears in the Middle East and beyond that Moscow would fall into the Sunni-Shia divide. True, Russia's allies on the ground were all Shia forces: the Alawite regime in Damascus; Iran and its ally Hezbollah and other Shiite formations; and the majority Shiite government in Baghdad. On the opposite side, there were all Sunni forces: the Syrian rebels, Islamic State, and Nusra. Moreover, the rebels were backed by Sunni powers, such as Turkey, Saudi Arabia, and Qatar. It looked like Russia's venture in the Middle East was totally a losing proposition.

In reality, it did not turn out that way. We have already discussed the roller-coaster relationship with Turkey that evolved toward a quasi-alliance. Very important, Moscow focused on Egypt, the key

Sunni country in the Arab world, which it sees as its central partner in the area. It cultivated Sunni monarchies, such as Jordan and the smaller Gulf States. Amman's participation in the Astana talks has been a major coup for Moscow. In Moscow or Sochi in 2015–2016, Putin hosted leaders of virtually all Arab countries. Even the Syrian Sunni opposition groups were not ignored by the Russian Foreign Ministry. To many Sunni countries, Russia's intervention in Syria also diminished the influence of Shiite Iran in Damascus, thus being the "lesser evil."

Within Russia, where Sunnis also make up a near-totality of indigenous Muslim population, Moscow sought to strengthen ties with leaders of Muslim-majority regions and mainstream clerics. Chechnya's head, Ramzan Kadyrov, was particularly helpful in the effort of presenting Russia's Syria campaign as a war on terrorists who had abandoned true Islam. The military police battalion sent to Aleppo in late 2016 was largely made up of Sunni Chechens. Mintimer Shaymiev, the former head of Tatarstan, a predominantly Muslim republic on the Volga, initiated the founding of an Islamic Academy in Kazan, to revive the tradition of Tatar Islamic theology and stem the flow of students from Russia to the more radicalized Islamic schools in the Arab world and Pakistan.

Diplomacy

Gulf States and Iran

While allied with Iran in Syria, Russia is not supportive of Tehran's regional agenda, whether in Syria, the Gulf, or in Yemen. Moscow is a major supplier of arms to Iran, but it has consistently indicated to Iran's Arab neighbors that it was willing to sell them arms, too. The Gulf States, of course, are mostly dependent on the United States and its European allies as providers of weapons systems. However, purchasing arms and military equipment is also purchasing a measure of political reassurance. Whatever their thoughts about Assad, it was not lost on Sunni Arab leaders that Moscow stood by its client through the grueling years of war, against all odds, while the United States, a long-time supporter of conservative Arab regimes, abandoned Hosni Mubarak when it concluded that he was doomed.

The very fact that Russia sells weapons to Tehran suggests that it has some leverage over its client. From the Russian perspective, there is nothing inconsistent with arming antagonists. Thus, Moscow arms both Armenia and Azerbaijan, locked for close to thirty years in a conflict over Nagorno-Karabakh. This position even allows Russia to act as a trusted intermediary, capable at least of preventing resumption of large-scale violence and cutting short the flare-ups that periodically occur. In a way, this is similar to the longtime U.S. policy of supplying weapons to Israel, on one hand, and Egypt and Saudi Arabia, on the other.

Moderating the Saudi-Iranian match for regional influence is a huge challenge, something that Russia can hardly manage. Moscow, however, did already act as an intermediary between Tehran and Riyadh in the all-important issue of stemming oil production to support the price of oil. In November 2016, Putin interceded between Supreme Leader Khamenei and King Salman to help them reach a compromise that allowed OPEC to come up with a joint stance.

In Yemen's ongoing civil war, which drew in, on opposite sides, the Saudis and smaller Gulf countries overtly and Iran covertly, Moscow has taken a neutral position. Even though it was often accused by the Saudis and Qataris of its own intervention in Syria, Russia did not respond too forcefully by pointing its finger at the Saudi actions in Yemen. Instead, Russia has been pleading for a political solution to the Yemeni war and a reconciliation of the warring parties. Iran is hardly pleased with this attitude, but there is nothing it can do about it. Russia is playing a bigger game in both the Middle East and beyond.

Diplomacy

Egypt: Mubarak, Morsi, and Sissi

From the start, Moscow's attitude toward Hosni Mubarak, who became president of Egypt in 1981, was far less hostile than to his predecessor Anwar Sadat. Over the years, the relationship between Moscow and Cairo, though never as close as in the times of Nasser, improved considerably. In 2011, the Kremlin did not cheer Mubarak's ouster at the hands of a popular revolt. While deploring spreading regional instability, Russia took a studiously neutral stance on the "Tahrir revolution" in Egypt, seeing it as a matter for Egyptians themselves.

When the free presidential elections in 2012 resulted in a victory for Mohammed Morsi, leader of the Muslim Brotherhood, Moscow again displayed pragmatism. It decided against ignoring the popularly elected leader and invited Morsi for a meeting with Putin. However, as Morsi was proving increasingly divisive and destabilizing within the country, the Kremlin supported the "forces of order" led by Field Marshal Abdelfattah al-Sissi. After the July 2013 military coup, Sissi, then defense minister and head of the military junta, was not only invited to meet with Putin, but publicly blessed by him to run for the presidency in the June 2014 presidential election, even before he made a formal announcement.

Putin and Sissi were united in seeing Islamist radicalism and extremism as the biggest security threat. This vision in turn changed Cairo's attitude toward the developments in Syria and Russia's military operation there. Winning Egypt's qualified support in Syria was a moral boost and a big achievement of Russia's diplomacy. Another big win, this time more on the material side, was resumption of Egyptian arms purchases from Russia and revival of military cooperation between the two countries. However, cash-strapped Cairo had to rely on Saudi Arabia and other rich Gulf countries for paying for Russian arms. Thus, Saudi Arabia and Russia, opposed to each other in Syria and on a number of other fronts, found themselves supporting the same regime in Egypt.

Libya's Warring Parties

Libya may have long been on the far periphery of Russia's regional policies, but at the end of World War II Stalin interestingly sought a UN trusteeship for the Soviet Union in Libya, heretofore an Italian possession. In conjunction with his other move, to get control of the Turkish Straits, this was probably part of a strategic design not only to get the keys to the entrance of the Black Sea, but also to acquire a base in the Mediterranean. Stalin's request on Libya was never granted, even as his demand on Turkey was thwarted, but both illustrate Moscow's long-term strategic intentions.

Russia was most critical of the Western governments' policies in Libya during the 2011 military intervention. Europeans and Americans were blamed for exceeding the UN Security Council mandate that Moscow had not blocked. Rather than saving civilian lives, Russians pointed out, they went ahead to change the regime. As a result of those policies, Libya has de facto ceased to exist as a state. Currently, Russia insists that the task of the international community in Libya is to defeat IS, Al Qaeda, and other extremists active in the country since the downfall of Qaddafi, and restoring the country's statehood. On the latter, it has its own ideas, but is open to collaborating with others.

Russia has grown skeptical of the UN-sponsored political process launched after the signature in December 2015 of the Skhirat accords. Moscow insists that the internationally recognized government in Tripoli led by Prime Minister Faiz Sarraj, which does not control much territory outside the capital, reach accommodation with the forces controlling eastern Libya out of Tobruk, headed by General Khalifa Haftar. Moscow maintains contacts with both, and invited Farraj for a visit in early 2017. However, it gives clear preference to General Haftar. In 2016, the eastern Libyan strongman, who studied in the Soviet Union and reportedly had asked for Moscow's military support, was invited aboard a Russian aircraft carrier for a videoconference with Defense Minister Sergei Shoigu.

Interestingly, Haftar's administration is also backed by Egypt, and his troops are supported by the United Arab Emirates air force. Russia's direct military intervention on Haftar's behalf was also discussed, but, for the time being, the Kremlin has decided against opening a second front in the Middle East after Syria. This small episode demonstrates the shifting nature of alliances and allegiances in the Middle East, where different situations result in very different combinations of protagonists. The Russians, with their vaunted pragmatism and a fair share of cynicism, appear well suited for this environment.

Another interesting development is Russia's open criticism of the "behind-the-back machinations" of the UN Secretary General's Special Representative for Libya, Martin Kobler. This vocal dissatisfaction is becoming part of a new pattern: Russia is voicing criticism of UN officials (the Special Representative for Syria, Staffan de Mistura, or the former UN Secretary General Ban Ki-Moon) who in its view are taking pro-Western stances. By making its criticisms and reservations public, Moscow has come forward to demand a more balanced mix of international officials. What Moscow is looking for in Libya is to be part of the eventual settlement, which would give it a share of lucrative contracts, erasing the losses sustained as a result of Qaddafi's ouster. To many in the United States and Europe, however, Russian activities in Libya look suspicious. Against the background of the Syria war and in connection with Moscow's expanding links with countries such as Turkey, Egypt, and Cyprus, they fear a nascent Russian "sphere of influence" in the Eastern Mediterranean. Geopolitical competition with Moscow is again accepted as a reality. The sad result is that, even in countries such as Libya, Syria, and Afghanistan where the West and Russia share important interests, such as rolling back extremism and enhancing stability, they find themselves increasingly as competitors pursuing agendas that almost exclude cooperation.

*

Once a rigid, zero-sum ideological and geopolitical player, Moscow has recently transformed itself into a paragon of pragmatism. It does not have either all-out allies or all-out adversaries anywhere in the region. Russia does not ignore the Middle East's treacherous divides: it knows that falling into them can be fatal. It seeks instead to straddle them, forming relationships with opposing parties on the basis of overlapping interests. Russia is busy promoting its own interests with all its partners, fully aware of those parties' own interests. To a significant degree, it works.

This does not mean that Russia is only using positive incentives in seeking to get its way. The Turkey episode (November 2015–July 2016) demonstrated its power to bring pressure to bear on a major regional country to make it change its course and cooperate with Russia on Moscow's terms. A major part of Russia's strategy to get Turkey back as a partner was the use of the Kurdish issue. Yet rather than betraying some of its partners to get what it wants from others, Moscow is seeking a balance that would maximize its gain without losing credibility with either party. Basically, it has learned to see Middle Eastern diplomacy as a bazaar where it has some valuable goods to sell, which it means to do for the highest price.

4

Trade

Russia's interests in the Middle East remain largely geopolitical and security-linked. Yet after the end of the Cold War there has been a clear expansion of market-based economic exchanges. Unlike the Soviet Union that went abroad to spend money on prestigious economic assistance projects such as the Aswan High Dam or Helwan Steel Mill in Egypt or the Euphrates Dam in Syria, the Russian Federation is primarily interested in making money abroad. Since 1991, the importance of the economic dimension in Russia's foreign relations has generally grown. This also applies to the Middle East, even though it trails far behind Russia's leading trading partners: the European Union, China, and the former Soviet states.

Russia's economy is relatively small, its GDP amounting to just about 1.5 to 2 percent of the

113

global total. After years of extensive growth powered by rising oil prices, Russia's economy ran out of steam by 2013, and then was severely buffeted by the plunging of oil prices in 2014–2015. Western sanctions, while having a limited impact on Russia's economy, essentially sent a chilling message across the world that Russia was a risky partner to do business with: those who dared to deal with Russia might have to answer to the United States. To be sure, Russia was not put in a position similar to Iran: its oil and gas were not barred from Western markets, but financial transactions via American banks faced additional scrutiny.

More fundamentally, Russia's external economic relations are limited by the current structure of the Russian economy. It is still heavily dependent on the energy sector. Whereas the Soviet Union had a vast industrial capacity, even if often lagging in quality in comparison to Western countries—this was often compensated by lower prices—Russia has relatively few goods and services to offer to its trading partners. It is highly competitive, however, in several important areas such as energy, arms, and grain. These goods find markets in the Middle East as well.

While the Middle East is not among Russia's major customers, its share of Russia's foreign trade has been growing, from 3.9 percent in 1995 to 6.6 percent in 2004 to 7 percent in 2015. Four-fifths of Russia's regional trade, however, is with the region's non-Arab countries: Turkey (accounting for almost 70 percent of the total figure), Iran, and Israel. Among the Arab trading partners, Egypt is in the lead (7 percent), followed by the Gulf Cooperation Council member states (6 percent), while Syria trails far behind (2 percent). Russian exports to the Arab world are mostly made up of energy products, metals, timber, and food. Machinery (excluding arms) only takes a modest share. Russian imports are dominated by fruit and vegetables and textiles.[1] As long as the Russian economy remains poorly diversified, this rather primitive structure of trade and economic relations will persist and limit economic exchanges. Yet in the key areas mentioned above, Russia's presence in the region is significant.

Arms

One of the world's leading arms exporters for over half a century, Russia is now second only to the United States. Moscow traditionally looks at the Middle East as a major market for its defense industry. As far back as the early twentieth century, the Russian Empire and the Soviet Union used to supply arms to the Shah of Iran. In the 1920s and the 1930s, Moscow delivered weapons to Turkey. Since the 1950s, Moscow has been a major supplier of arms and military equipment to a number of Arab countries, from Algeria to Yemen. While Israel purchased arms from the West—Britain, France, and the United States—its Arab foes turned to the Soviet Union. In the days of the Cold War, Moscow's arms relations to the Arab countries were closely linked to its strategic considerations and ideology, and these did not always result in financial gain. When the USSR broke apart, Syria and Iraq owed Moscow $13 billion each, and Libya owed $4.5 billion, mostly for weapons transfers. In the 2000s, Moscow agreed to write off most of these debts in exchange for new contracts, which would be paid for with real money.

Currently, Russia's military-technological presence in the region is a far cry from the Soviet days. Other than those involved in the Syrian civil war, the number of Russian technical personnel active in the Arab countries' armed forces, and the number of Arab officers undergoing training in Russia, has gone down by an order of magnitude. The upside is that now Moscow's clients are paying. Russia's political reentry into the region helps to win more contracts. The ongoing Russian military operation in Syria is likely to boost the prestige of Russian-made weapons and further advertise the value of Moscow's politico-military backing.

As the following brief summary of military-technical cooperation (as it is known in Russia) in the Middle East suggests, Moscow is coming back to its traditional markets and is entering new ones.

Egypt used to be Moscow's principal arms client from 1955 until 1974, when President Sadat's reversal of alliances pushed it largely to buy from the U.S. arms industry. Low-level arms purchases from Russia, however, never stopped, even in 1991. Under Hosni Mubarak, himself a pilot trained in the Soviet Union, Russia in the 2000s supplied Egypt with Tor-M1 and Buk air defense systems, Igla portable anti-aircraft missiles, and Mi-8 and Mi-17 helicopters.[2] The planned purchase of the MiG-29 fighters, however, was stopped at U.S. insistence. By now, Soviet- and Russian-made weapons account for about 60 percent of the Egyptian military arsenal.

With the arrival of Field Marshal Abdelfattah Sissi in power in 2013, Egypt's arms relationship with Russia has expanded considerably. The two countries began holding regular joint meetings of defense and foreign ministers. The suspension of U.S. military assistance to Cairo as a sign of Washington's disapproval of the military takeover by the Egyptian army further strengthened the relationship with Moscow. Politically, the two countries drew closer together, particularly with regard to the conflicts in Syria and Libya. In June 2015, the first Russian-Egyptian joint naval exercise was held in the Mediterranean; in 2016, special operations forces of the two countries trained together. In September 2016 Russian defense minister Shoigu called Egypt Russia's "most important strategic partner" in the Middle East and North Africa.

Syria, which also used to be a major client in Soviet times, lost this position due to the change in the geopolitical situation. The end of the Cold War coincided with the fundamental improvement of Moscow's relations with Israel. In this new situation, Damascus was either unable or unwilling to repay its Soviet-era debt. From 1991 to 2011, Syria concluded contracts worth under $1 billion, purchasing mainly Pantsyr S-1 and Buk M2 air defense systems and anti-tank weapons. The circumstances changed again, dramatically, with the advent of the Arab Spring.

After the beginning of the Syrian uprising in 2011, which soon morphed into a civil war, Russia delivered to Damascus another $1 billion worth of arms and ammunition, mostly for the purposes of fighting insurgents.[3] In 2016, Russia also transferred to Damascus about ten modernized Su-24 M2 bombers.[4] Much more important, of course, was direct Russian military intervention in Syria. Yet throughout the entire history of the relationship, Syria has never been a lucrative arms market to Russia. What it was and what it remains is a crucially important geopolitical position in the region that keeps Moscow intensely interested.

Iraq, another major Soviet client since the 1960s, purchased a lot of weapons from Moscow during the war with Iran in the 1980s. The arms relationship was discontinued after Iraq's 1990 invasion of Kuwait. Later, Baghdad came completely under U.S. influence as a result of the 2003 American invasion and the toppling of the regime of Saddam Hussein. Yet, as in the case of Egypt, Afghanistan, or Libya, U.S.-provided arms did not completely ease out Russian weaponry, which remained competitive due to its relative simplicity in operation and lower price. This relates to Su-25 ground attack planes, Mi-8, Mi-17, Mi-28, and Mi-35M helicopters, the Pantsyr-S1 air defense system, and TOS-1 multiple rocket launchers, which Iraq ordered in 2012–2014 to become the major Russian client in the Middle East.[5] This was a big step for Moscow, not only in reconquering the seemingly lost market in an oil-rich country, but in winning a de facto ally in the region. In 2015, Iraq joined Iran and Russia in a coalition to support Damascus against the rebels and the Islamic State group.

Iran, unlike its Arab neighbors, only began purchasing Soviet arms on a large scale in the years 1989–1991. These included MiG-29 fighters, Su-24 MK bombers, S-200 air defense systems, and Class 877 submarines. In addition, T-72 tanks and BMP-2 armored personnel carriers were assembled in Iran under a Soviet license. In the late 1990s, however, Moscow had to suspend the relationship under pressure from Washington, concerned about Iran's nuclear and missile programs and regional ambitions. This concession to the United States produced humiliation among the defense industrial community in Russia and cost Moscow its credibility with Iran.

The arms transfers resumed with the arrival in the Kremlin of Vladimir Putin. Since 2000, Iran has bought or intends to buy a wide range of Russian weaponry: Su-25 and Su-30 SM fighters, Mi-8MT and Mi-17 helicopters, Tor-M1 air defense systems, and Bastion coastal batteries with Yakhont missiles.[6] In this way, Russia has become Iran's most important source of weapons purchases. In 2016, Russia finally delivered to Iran all four units of the highly capable S-300 PMU2 air defense system, which it had agreed to supply in 2007 but then stopped the transfer in 2010 in conjunction with the UN Security Council's sanctions against Iran. After the conclusion in 2015 of the JCPOA agreement on Iran's nuclear program, Moscow lifted its ban that had jarred the relationship between the two countries for several years. This move made Russia the first weapons supplier to Iran after the conclusion of the JCPOA.[7]

Russia's arms relations with the **Gulf States** were first established in the 1990s, when the **United Arab Emirates** and **Kuwait** bought BMP-3 armored personnel carriers and Smerch multiple rocket launchers. The UAE also purchased the Pantsyr S-1 air defense system in order to diversify its armory. For its part, the UAE is cooperating with Russia's defense industry in developing drones, an area where Russia is lagging behind. There have also been discussions about a UAE welfare fund investing in "Helicopters of Russia," a Rostec company. There is even some talk of a joint aircraft development. At this point, however, these are only token gestures or rumors. The Gulf monarchies remain virtually completely dependent on U.S. and West European weaponry. This fully applies to Saudi Arabia.

The Russians have long been looking at the **Saudi** market, offering Riyadh T-90 tanks, BMP-3 APCs, Mi-17 and Mi-35 helicopters, and air defense systems, but so far without success. Even though the Saudis are diversifying their foreign relations away from their formerly near-total reliance on Washington, they are still too cautious even to begin token purchases of Russian arms. Over time, this may change. Ideology is no longer an issue, and the strategic landscape keeps changing. Since the 1970s, Moscow has been a supplier of weapons— mostly anti-tank and air defense systems, as well as helicopters—to **Jordan**. On the opposite end of the Arabian Peninsula, **Yemen** has been a traditional buyer of Russian arms, such as MiG-29 fighters, Mi-17 helicopters, and BMP-2 APCs, purchased often with the Gulf States' money—as is now also the case of Egypt.

Then there is defense industrial cooperation with **Israel**. This is a wholly different kind of relationship compared to that with the Arab countries. Israel does not buy weapons from Moscow. The Russians, however, were unpleasantly surprised when Israeli-made drones were used by the Georgian forces during the brief war in the Caucasus in 2008. Since then, Moscow has been buying Israeli technology to improve its own domestic drone production. The defense relationship is tied in with broad strategic understanding between Russia and Israel. In 2014, after Crimea and Donbass, when Israel refused to join the U.S.-led sanctions regime against Russia, the Jewish state has become a near-unique source of advanced technology for Moscow. Israel, of course, is not shy to use this leverage in its dealings with Russia.

Russian arms transfers to **Turkey**, a NATO member, resumed after many decades, though on a very limited scale, in the early 1990s when Moscow provided Ankara with BTR-80 APCs. In the 2000s, Turkey was considering purchasing Russian-made S-300 air defense systems similar to those Greece, another NATO member state, bought to be deployed in Cyprus. In the end, however, it was the Chinese system that was chosen to help defend Turkey's airspace. In early 2017, after the normalization of the bilateral relationship, the conversation was restarted, only this time with regard to the more capable S-400 system.

Libya, under Muammar Qaddafi, used to be a major purchaser of arms from the Soviet Union and European countries, mainly France and Italy. Once the economic sanctions imposed on Libya after the Lockerbie airplane bombing were lifted in 2006, Moscow signed major contracts with Tripoli,

which included transfer of twelve SU-30 MK2
fighters, twelve MiG-29 SMT fighters, the S-300
PMU2 and Tor-M1 air defense systems, and Class
636 submarines. The toppling of Qaddafi in 2011
prevented the full implementation of the deal, but
Moscow remains hopeful that when Libya stabilizes
internally, the oil-rich country may return as an
arms market. The special relationship that Moscow
maintains with General Khalifa Khaftar points in
that direction.

In the mid-2000s, it was **Algeria** that became the
Arab champion in purchasing arms from Russia.
It signed an arms deal with Moscow worth $8
billion. With that, Algeria became Russia's third
biggest arms client worldwide, behind only China
and India. The package includes Su-30 MKI(A) and
MiG-29 SMT/UBT fighters, S-300 PMU2 air defense
systems, T-90 main battle tanks (100 vehicles in
2016 alone), Class 636 submarines, and a range of
other weapons for the army, navy, and the air force.
There are reports[8] that Algeria is also buying 12
Su-32 (a version of Su-34) bombers. Once Algeria's
rearmament is completed, the country will continue
to depend on Russia for maintenance, modernization, and new arms. Since Algeria's independence
from France in 1962, the country has been buying
arms mostly from Moscow.

Russia's own $700 billion rearmament program, begun in 2011, is due to be completed by 2020. It may be extended beyond that date, as a number of projects have been rescheduled to trim spending. After 2020, Russia will also purchase more weapons than it did prior to 2010. However, going forward, the Russian defense industry's revenues will depend more on foreign military sales. This is where the Middle East comes in as a major market.

Energy

In the Middle East, Russia, whose exports are mostly energy products, has to deal with countries, many of whom are also energy producers. In other words, Russia does not need oil and gas from the Middle East, and cannot sell its own hydrocarbons there. This naturally reduces Russia's economic role in the Middle East, but at the same time it makes Moscow an important partner in regulating supply to the world market and thus in setting the price for the region's main export product.

Russia, a leading independent oil producer, is not a member of OPEC, and its relations with the cartel have been rocky. Yet, in late 2016, after a failed attempt earlier in the year, which fell through due to Iran's unwillingness to join, Putin personally managed to broker an accord, which then held as agreed. It first helped engineer a deal within OPEC, between Iran and Saudi Arabia, and then between OPEC as a whole and non-OPEC producers. As a result, oil production was cut, including by Russia itself, and oil prices rose. This was a major achievement of the Kremlin's energy diplomacy.

Another coup achieved in December 2016 was the decision by Qatar's sovereign welfare fund to buy a 19.5 percent share in the Russian largely state-owned company Rosneft. This decision was made despite the sharp differences between Moscow and Doha on Syria and the U.S. policy of sanctions against Russia. Potentially this constitutes a major breakthrough in attracting Gulf States' investment in Russia. The Rosneft deal was followed in 2017 by Qatar's publicly expressed interest in buying shares in Novatek, Russia's independent gas producer. After Russia has repaid its 1991 debt to Kuwait, its Fund of Direct Investment is eyeing the Gulf States as potential investors. To make itself more attractive to them, Moscow is making first steps toward allowing Islamic finance in Russia.

A few Russian companies have long been present in the Middle East, but their activities there are very dependent on the political developments. After the U.S. invasion of Iraq in 2003, Lukoil, which had a major interest in North Rumaila, found itself at a disadvantage with the new authorities in Baghdad. As Russia's relations with Iran soured in 2010, Lukoil and Gazprom Neft withdrew from Iran, while Gazprom stopped its activity at South Pars. Only Tatneft was allowed to stay.[9] In Egypt, by contrast, Lukoil produces one-sixth of that country's oil. (Egypt, of course, is not a major oil producer.) Rosneft delivers oil products to Egypt, and Gazprom has a contract to deliver liquefied natural gas there.

Russia, Iran, and Qatar are the world's top producers of natural gas. Political differences among these countries, however, have not allowed them so far to coordinate their policies. The idea of a "gas OPEC," first broached by Putin in 2002, has not been implemented. Instead, a Gas Exporting Countries Forum was constituted in 2008 in Moscow. Russia had hoped that the headquarters of the forum would be established in St. Petersburg, but Iran's last-minute change of position resulted in Doha being chosen instead. The forum is a consultative body, a veritable "non-OPEC."

Russia, which is a major supplier of gas to Europe, does not welcome potential Iranian exports to the European Union. Western sanctions against Iran were in fact in Gazprom's interests. Qatar's plans to build a gas pipeline to Syria's Mediterranean coast were rejected by Damascus, which in 2011 preferred a similar project proposed by Iran instead. Either pipeline would be a competitor for Gazprom, but neither is likely to be implemented as long as the Syrian conflict is not resolved. Meanwhile, Gazprom is looking for gas offshore near the Syrian coast. It has also advanced an idea to lay a gas pipeline to Israel.

Gazprom's most important customer in the region is, of course, Turkey. Since the 1990s, Russia has been supplying Turkey with gas via the Blue Stream pipeline laid across the Black Sea from Novorossiysk to Samsun. An expansion of the Blue Stream ran into trouble when Turkey began considering support for a rival Nabucco project, designed to supply Europe with gas from Azerbaijan and Turkmenistan. However, Russian plans in 2009–2014 to build the South Stream pipeline to supply southern Europe by going around Ukraine were blocked by the European Union and the United States, which had concerns about Europe becoming too dependent on Russia as an energy supplier.

After the Ukraine crisis, Moscow officially gave up the South Stream project and came up with an idea of a Turkish Stream, a pipeline that would go from Russia to Turkey, from which the Europeans would be expected to take gas for their own needs. It is not clear how Europe eventually responds to that option and whether Russia actually stops moving its export gas through Ukraine when the current transit contract expires in 2019. Turkey certainly wishes to play the role of an energy hub to Europe, and views Russia as one of its key partners in it.

Apart from oil and gas, Russia is a major force in nuclear energy. For Rosatom and Atomstroiexport, the region accounts for more than half of their portfolio: $61 billion out of $110 billion. Russia first entered the Middle East nuclear market in Iran, where in 1995 it undertook to complete building the Bushehr nuclear reactor that the German company Siemens had to give up in 1980 due to sanctions. Bushehr 1, which became fully operational in 2012, is to be followed by Bushehr 2, whose building was started in 2016, and Bushehr 3, planned for 2018.

Next to Iran, Russia in 2010 concluded a contract to build a nuclear power plant at Akkuyu in Turkey, whose first stage is to be completed by 2020. This is the world's first project concluded on the build-own-operate model. The project survived the political storm in Russian-Turkish relations in 2015–2016, and was reconfirmed at the March 2017 summit meeting in Moscow. In the Arab world, Rosatom

Trade

has undertaken to build nuclear power stations in Jordan and Egypt. Both projects involve substantial Russian financing. In Jordan, Rosatom finances 49.9 percent of the project; to Egypt, Russia made a loan covering 85 percent of the $25 billion cost of the El Dabaa project.[10] Financial burdens that Rosatom has to carry are compounded by political issues when it comes to discussing potential projects in such countries as the United Arab Emirates or Saudi Arabia. Rosatom has to be patient.

Other Economic Exchanges

Apart from arms and nuclear power, grain exports are an important item in Russia's trade with the Middle East. Reduced to the role of a heavy importer of grain in the late Soviet period, Russia in the 2000s has recovered its role as a major grain producer and exporter. To Egypt alone, it sells 4.5 million tons of grain, accounting for two-fifths of the grain imports of that most populous Arab country. When Russia in 2009 temporarily suspended exports due to poor harvest, this led to a hike in global food prices.

In 1972, Anwar Sadat expelled 20,000 Soviet military personnel from Egypt. Almost forty years later, in 2011, as his successor Hosni Mubarak was toppled by the January 26 revolution, Russia had to evacuate double that number of vacationers stranded on the beaches of Hurghada and Sharm el-Sheikh. The two figures illustrate, in a nutshell, the story of Russia's involvement in the Middle East. Undeterred by the domestic complications in Egypt, in 2014, 3.2 million Russian tourists went to Egypt, accounting for about a third of all foreign visitors in Egypt. It was only the bombing in October 2015 of a Russian passenger plane en route from Sharm el-Sheikh to St. Petersburg that led to a suspension of Russian package tours to Egypt, which have not yet been allowed to restart.

Almost simultaneously, the downing of the Russian bomber by Turkey led to a temporary halt to charter flights to that country. By early 2016, the number of Russian tourists in Turkey decreased by a factor of six. This came as a very heavy blow to the Turkish tourist industry and played a role in President Erdogan's decision to seek reconciliation with Putin. The relationship repaired in mid-2016: Russians are flocking back, although the height of the Russian tourist presence in Turkey—3.5 million—has not yet been reached, due in part to the recession that hit Russia in 2014. Egypt and Turkey are the top two destinations, and both are heavily dependent on revenues from Russian tourism, but other countries such as Israel, Cyprus, Tunisia, and the UAE are also attracting thousands of Russians looking for a spot in the sun near warm seas. To help them there, communities of Russians employed by the local tourist industries have sprung up. At Egyptian resorts only, they number about 7,000. Through these contacts, the Middle East has become much closer to the Russian public than ever before.

Most talk about geo-economics of Eurasia today is about the Silk Road Economic Belt, which runs from China to Europe. Russia is seeking to harmonize its own integration arrangement, the Eurasian Economic Union (EEU), with China's plans. At the same time, however, the Russians are hoping to build meridional connections along the North-South axis. One corridor would run from Mumbai to St. Petersburg across Iran, Azerbaijan, and the Caspian Sea. Other corridors would link Russia's Novorossiysk port on the Black Sea to the ports in the eastern Mediterranean. In Egypt, Russians are planning an industrial zone to serve as a gateway for Russian exports to Africa, while UAE has invested in a Russian port at Ust-Luga in the Baltic, near St. Petersburg. At this point, much of this is only developing or appears far-fetched, but this can be a way to the future.

Moscow views the EEU as an open project. Rather than confining the union to the former Soviet republics, the Russians are looking at open free-trade arrangements with a number of partners. In Asia, this is China, Vietnam, and other members of the Association of Southeast Asian Nations. In the Middle East, Moscow is looking, above all, at Turkey, Israel, and Egypt. At this point, however, Russia is only making baby steps at fostering economic integration outside the former Soviet Union.

*

Even though Russia's economic role in the Middle East is modest, the current pattern of exchanges points to much more interaction between it and the countries of the region than there used to be in the days of the Soviet Union. Arms, energy—both fossil and nuclear—as well as grain and tourism are the key areas where Russia is a big player even now. Real integration, however, can only be achieved when and if infrastructure projects linking the north and south of Greater Eurasia are implemented. In other words, this would be when the China-led East-West axis is complemented by South-North links, bringing together the Middle East, on one hand, with Russia, on the other. At this point, it looks to be a very long-term proposition.

Conclusions

Russia does not have a grand strategy for the Middle East, but its return to the region is of strategic importance for itself and a significant international development. It is not just a return to an important region, but a comeback to the global scene after a twenty-five-year absence. This breakthrough for Russia's foreign policy has contributed to the ongoing change of the global order—away from U.S. dominance and back to some sort of a balance of power among several major players, including Russia. Moscow has demonstrated that a combination of a clear sense of objective, strong political will, area expertise and experience, resourceful diplomacy, a capable military, plus an ability to coordinate one's actions with partners and situational allies in a very diverse and highly complex region can go a long way to help project power onto the top level.

Conclusions

This was exactly what Putin was aiming for. His main foreign policy objective has been to bring Russia back to the top level of global politics, and he chose the Middle East as the area for that breakthrough. So far, Moscow has been successful in its daring and risky endeavor, which is still continuing, but risks and dangers certainly abound. The Kremlin's initial objective of nominally reentering the top echelon of powerful geopolitical actors achieved, Putin now faces a different task, to sustain the momentum and convert Russia's presence into lasting public goods that can only confirm the newly restored prestige of a great power. One obvious example should be a durable peace settlement in Syria; another, managing relations with competing regional powers: Turkey, Iran, Israel, Saudi Arabia, and Egypt.

To achieve either objective, Russia will need to cooperate with regional and global partners. It has been able to create a diplomatic coalition with Turkey and Iran, which is crucial for keeping the ceasefire in place, but it needs to reach out to the Saudis and the Qataris to ensure a productive diplomatic process, as well as to the Egyptians to give it gravitas in the Arab world, and to the United States to get on board and be able to claim a formal co-equal status as a global peacemaker. The United

States is also Russia's prime partner in breaking the IS stranglehold on parts of northern and central Syria. Achieving a form of partnership with the United States on terms acceptable to Moscow has been and remains the chief goal of Russia's intervention in Syria.

What Russia could also do, at the appropriate moment, is help resume the Israeli-Palestinian peace process. As one power with good relations with Israel and both Palestinian entities—the Palestinian Authority in the West Bank/Ramallah and Hamas in Gaza—it can try to get things moving again, even if the expectations should be held in check. It is important to stress that any Russian contribution to finding elusive resolution to the seventy-year-old Israeli-Palestinian dispute is made and presented as part of the collective effort by the Middle East Quartet, and in coordination with the other three members, the United States, the United Nations, and the European Union.

With the Trump administration in the United States very suspicious of Iran's ambitions, the nuclear agreement between Iran and the international community, the JCPOA, may be in danger of unraveling. American-Iranian relations may again deteriorate to the point of crisis. Russia, which has long been an advocate of a political solution of the issues related to Iran's nuclear program, is likely to play a major role in seeking to preserve the international accord and preventing renewed confrontation close to its borders. This may be the next big test for Russian diplomacy in the region. Another test will come if and when the United States decides to end its military involvement in Afghanistan, which will then become more of a problem for the neighboring countries, and for Moscow.

Russia's exercise of power, whether military or economic, in the region is limited not so much by its own ambitions as by the country's available economic and financial resources. In order to be a more important player in the region, Russia would need to be much more than an arms supplier to several countries. Energy policy coordination, especially with Saudi Arabia and Iran, is one area where Moscow's influence can grow. Another area is infrastructure development, linking Russia with the Middle East along the North-South axis, across the Black Sea, the Caspian, and the Caucasus. Tapping into the financial resources of the Gulf States is certainly of interest, as is technological cooperation with Israel and the UAE and industrial cooperation with Turkey, Iran, and Egypt.

As Russia said goodbye in 2014 to the two principal foreign policy concepts that had guided it since the downfall of the Soviet Union—its own integration into an enlarged West and reintegration of the former Soviet borderlands into a greater Russia—it began looking for a new frame of reference. Three years on, it appears that it has found the answer. Russia sees itself as a major single unit unto itself, with global connections and a basic freedom of action. Neither "western" nor "eastern," it occupies virtually all the north and much of the center of the great continent of Eurasia. Positioned that way, Russia treats virtually everyone else as a neighbor, from Norway to North Korea.

The Middle East is very much part of that greater Eurasian neighborhood, where Moscow seeks to build a system of international relations no longer dominated by the United States and not to be overshadowed by a single "local" hegemon, China. Moscow's moves in the Middle East are not designed primarily to dislodge America's influence: what Russia wants from Washington, essentially, is respect and cooperation. The relationship, however, is likely to be essentially adversarial. More to the point, Russia hopes to create an equilibrium between itself and China, Moscow's principal partner in the emerging Greater Eurasia. By acting swiftly and resolutely now, the Kremlin is buying time, compensating for its obvious economic weakness with political acumen and military effectiveness. Competition in Eurasia, however, must and will go on, and its result will be decided by the fundamentals, not tactical agility.

There, Russian leaders have their work cut out for them. They need to finally come up with a model of economic development that works: they have to revive the country's technological and scientific potential; work even harder to address the looming demographic problems; and, of course, preserve political stability in the country even as the prospect of power transition emerges on the horizon. These leaders will need both vision and clear goals, as well as a keen sense of the future, not only pride in the old glory.

Notes

Chapter 1 History

1 V. P. Potemkin (ed.), *Istoria diplomatii*. Moscow: OGIZ Publishers, 1945, v. 3, p. 33.

2 Igor Delanoe, *Russie. Les enjeux du retour au Moyen-Orient. L'Inventaire/L'Observatoire franco-russe*. Moscow, 2016, p. 32.

3 Ivan Serov, *Zapiski iz chemodana*. Moscow: Prosveshchenie, 2017, p. 547.

4 Maj. Gen. V. A. Zolotarev (ed.), *Rossiya (SSSR) v lokalnykh voynakh I voennykh konfliktakh vtoroy poloviny XX veka*. Moscow: Kuchkovo Pole, 2000, p. 180.

5 Ibid., pp. 190–196.

6 Ibid., p. 209.

7 General Secretary Leonid Brezhnev's Report to the 26th Congress of the Communist Party of the Soviet Union, February 23, 1981. Moscow: Politzdat, 1981.

8 Zolotarev (ed.), *Rossiya (SSSR)*, pp. 210–211.

9 For Primakov's views and reflections on Moscow's policies toward the Middle East, see his *Russia and the Arabs: Behind the Scenes in the Middle East from the Cold War to the Present*. New York: Basic Books, 2009.

10 *Kommersant*, January 29, 1993.

11 Vitaly Naumkin, Vliyanie, "Arabskoy vesny" 2011 g. na globalnuyu mezhdunarodnuyu sistemu. *Russia in Global Affairs*, July–August 2011.

12 See, e.g., President Dmitry Medvedev's remarks in Vladikavkaz on February 22, 2011, and Vice Prime Minister Igor Sechin's interview with the *Wall Street Journal*, February 21, 2011.

13 At a press conference in Paris during his 2012 visit.

14 Obama first called for Assad's departure as early as August 2011. See Scott Wilson and Joby Warrick, "Assad Must Go, Obama Says." *Washington Post*, August 18, 2011.

1 V. P. Potemkin (ed.), *Istoria diplomatii*. Moscow: OGIZ Publishers, 1945, v. 3, p. 33.

2 Igor Delanoe, *Russie. Les enjeux du retour au Moyen-Orient. L'Inventaire/L'Observatoire franco-russe*. Moscow, 2016, p. 32.

3 Ivan Serov, *Zapiski iz chemodana*. Moscow: Prosveshchenie, 2017, p. 547.

4 Maj. Gen. V. A. Zolotarev (ed.), *Rossiya (SSSR) v lokalnykh voynakh I voennykh konfliktakh vtoroy poloviny XX veka*. Moscow: Kuchkovo Pole, 2000, p. 180.

5 Ibid., pp. 190–196.

6 Ibid., p. 209.

Notes

General Secretary Leonid Brezhnev's Report to the 26th Congress of the Communist Party of the Soviet Union, February 23, 1981. Moscow: Politzdat, 1981.

8 Zolotarev (ed.), *Rossiya (SSSR)*, pp. 210–211.

9 For Primakov's views and reflections on Moscow's policies toward the Middle East, see his *Russia and the Arabs: Behind the Scenes in the Middle East from the Cold War to the Present*. New York: Basic Books, 2009.

10 *Kommersant*, January 29, 1993.

11 Vitaly Naumkin, Vliyanie, "Arabskoy vesny" 2011 g. na globalnuyu mezhdunarodnuyu sistemu. *Russia in Global Affairs*, July–August 2011.

12 See, e.g., President Dmitry Medvedev's remarks in Vladikavkaz on February 22, 2011, and Vice Prime Minister Igor Sechin's interview with the *Wall Street Journal*, February 21, 2011.

13 At a press conference in Paris during his 2012 visit.

14 Obama first called for Assad's departure as early as August 2011. See Scott Wilson and Joby Warrick, "Assad Must Go, Obama Says." *Washington Post*, August 18, 2011.

Chapter 2 War

1 Soviet arms transfers to Syria from 1957 to 1991 amounted to $26 billion. In 2005, Moscow wrote off $10 billion, or roughly three-quarters, of the out-

standing Syrian debt (M. Yu. Shepovalenko, *Siriysky rubezh*. Moscow: CAST, 2016, p. 17).

2 Delanoe, *Russie*, p. 68.
3 Shepovalenko, *Siriysky rubezh*, p. 89.
4 Uzbekistan's founding president, Islam Karimov, did pass away in September 2016.
5 Putin's address to the UN General Assembly, September 28, 2015.
6 About 20 million strong, mostly Sunni, one-seventh of the Russian population, and growing.
7 Shepovalenko, *Siriysky rubezh*, pp. 106–107.
8 Ibid., pp. 107–108.
9 Lavrov's public comment in New York, late September 2015.
10 Shepovalenko, *Siriysky rubezh*, p. 119.
11 Lavrov on the alliance with Syria.
12 Mikhail Khodaryonok, on Soloviev's nightly show, December 2016.
13 *Kommersant*, March 6, 2017.
14 Lavrov, May 4, 2016.

Chapter 4 Trade

1 Vitaly Naumkin, "Arabskoy vesny," p. 236.
2 Yu. N. Zinin, "Rossiysko-egipetskie otnosheniya vchera I segodnya." In *Mezhdunarodnaya analitika*. Moscow: IMI MGIMO 3 (17) (2016): p. 40.
3 Eksport vooruzheniy, issue 6, 2016, p. 9.
4 Ibid., p. 8.

Notes

5 Delanoe, *Russie*, pp. 36–37.
6 Ibid., pp. 38–40.
7 Eksport vooruzheniy, issue 6, 2016, p. 7.
8 Ibid., pp. 7, 9.
9 Vitaly Naumkin, "Arabskoy vesny," p. 238.
10 Zinin, "Rossiysko-egipetskie otnosheniya vchera I segodnya," p. 39.